Your Child's Social and Emotional Well-Being

Your Child's Social and Emotional Well-Being

A Complete Guide for Parents and Those Who Help Them

John S. Dacey, Lisa B. Fiore, and Steven Brion-Meisels

WILEY Blackwell

This edition first published 2016
© 2016 John Wiley & Sons, Ltd.

Registered Office
John Wiley & Sons, Ltd, The Atrium, Southern Gate, Chichester, West Sussex, PO19 8SQ, UK

Editorial Offices
350 Main Street, Malden, MA 02148-5020, USA
9600 Garsington Road, Oxford, OX4 2DQ, UK
The Atrium, Southern Gate, Chichester, West Sussex, PO19 8SQ, UK

For details of our global editorial offices, for customer services, and for information about how to apply for permission to reuse the copyright material in this book please see our website at www.wiley.com/wiley-blackwell.

Library of Congress Cataloging-in-Publication Data

Names: Dacey, John S., author. | Fiore, Lisa B., 1970– author. | Brion-Meisels, Steven, author.
Title: Your child's social and emotional well-being : a complete guide for parents
   and those who help them / John S. Dacey, Lisa B. Fiore, and Steven Brion-Meisels.
Description: Chichester, West Sussex, UK : John Wiley & Sons, 2016. |
   Includes bibliographical references and index.
Identifiers: LCCN 2015047274 (print) | LCCN 2016002683 (ebook) |
   ISBN 9781118977064 (hardback) | ISBN 9781118977057 (paperback) | ISBN 9781118976234 (ePub) |
   ISBN 9781118977040 (Adobe PDF)
Subjects: LCSH: Social skills in children. | Social skills–Study and teaching. | Home and school. |
   Child development. | BISAC: PSYCHOLOGY / Education & Training.
Classification: LCC BF723.S62 D33 2016 (print) | LCC BF723.S62 (ebook) | DDC 649/.7–dc23
LC record available at http://lccn.loc.gov/2015047274

A catalogue record for this book is available from the British Library.

Cover image: Getty Images © DragonImages

Set in 10.5/13pt Minion by SPi Global, Pondicherry, India
Printed and bound in Malaysia by Vivar Printing Sdn Bhd

1   2016

*This book is lovingly dedicated to the memory of
Dr. Steven Brion-Meisels—a dear friend, teacher, and source of
inspiration to thousands of his students, family, and friends. Steven's
wisdom contributed to the formation of this book, and his spirit
has gently guided our work since his passing in March 2014.
With deep gratitude, dear friend: John and Lisa.*

Contents

Acknowledgments

We have been graciously facilitated by the excellent personnel at Wiley Blackwell: Darren Reed, Senior Commissioning Editor; Karen Shield, Senior Project Editor, Psychology Books; and Amy Minshull, Social Sciences and Humanities, and to Janet Moth, Project Manager. Thanks also to our favorite elementary school teacher, Nancy Alloway, and to Lisa Doucette.

We got wonderful help from our Boston College undergraduate students: Emily Atkinson, John Bok, Elsa Hellberg, Patrick Genovese, Rosmailyn Lantigua, Seong Lee, Riccardo Moauro, Samantha Rodriguez, Tyler Schaeffer, and Jack Staid. Thanks for help "above and beyond."

Finally, each of us wants to recognize the contributions from our spouses, Linda Dacey, Ph.D., Stephen Fiore, Esq., and Linda Brion-Meisels, Ph.D. You're the greatest!

About the Companion Website

This book is accompanied by a companion website:

www.wiley.com/go/daceywellbeing

The website includes:
- extra resources including videos

1

All Children *Need* Social and Emotional Well-being

The survival of the human race depends at least as much on the cultivation of social and emotional intelligence as it does on the development of technological knowledge and skills.[1]

The need to refocus American schools on the holistic development of children is profound. One national survey discovered, for example, that among 148,000 middle and high school students, well under half felt they had developed social competencies such as empathy, decision-making, and conflict resolution skills. Only 29% indicated that their school provided caring, encouraging environments. Other research has found that as many as 60% of students become chronically disengaged from school, and 30% of high school students engage in multiple high risk behaviors such as substance abuse, sexual activity, violence, and attempted suicide.[2]

"Refocus schools on the holistic development of children"? The rising tide of dysfunctional behaviors throughout the world clearly supports social and emotional, as well as academic, learning.[3] Unfortunately, joining these

[1] Darling-Hammond, 2015, p. xi.
[2] Durlak et al., 2011, p. 405.
[3] e.g., Levine, 2013.

Your Child's Social and Emotional Well-Being: A Complete Guide for Parents and Those Who Help Them, First Edition. John S. Dacey, Lisa B. Fiore, and Steven Brion-Meisels.
© 2016 John Wiley & Sons, Ltd. Published 2016 by John Wiley & Sons, Ltd.
Companion website: www.wiley.com/go/daceywellbeing

three goals is not likely to be pursued any time soon. The "whole child" and "well-being" are objectives most parents favor for their children, but not if they get in the way of going to a good college or getting a good job. Since teaching for holistic well-being tends to take time from academic learning, it is most often remanded to the back burner of the educational stove.

Let's take a closer look at well-being, which refers to "the psychological capacity to cope with the demands arising across time, circumstances, and setting." In this book, we call training for well-being "social and emotional learning (SEL)." In international education, SEL is known by a variety of names: "education for mutual understanding," "peace education," "values education," "multicultural/intercultural education," "human rights education," "life skills," "citizenship, humanitarian or emotional education," "emotional intelligence," and "education for sustainable development."[4] Depending on the area of the world, the meaning of SEL also differs somewhat:

> Whereas Europe and Latin America commonly emphasize [SEL] links with human rights, Asia and sub-Saharan Africa highlight connections with a return to indigenous, cultural and religious values. Other differences exist across countries, such as a strong focus on the importance of citizenship education in enhancing national economic productivity in some places, and the role of citizenship education and the prevention of aggression and violence in others.[5]

We distinguish SEL from the other educational goal most societies have: academic learning (AL). AL refers to learning the knowledge and skills of the several subject-matter areas (math, science, etc.). We wish both SEL and AL would take place in schools everywhere. However, with so many countries concentrating on teaching and measuring AL, this goal appears unlikely. Therefore, we believe that for the most part, SEL will have to be fostered by parents and other adult members of the family.

Most of us agree on what social/emotional traits we want our children to learn in life. They need to:

- Know who they are and be mindful of the repercussions of their actions.
- Control themselves and make good judgments.

---

[4]   Torrente et al., 2015, p. 566.
[5]   Torrente et al., 2015, p. 567.

- Refrain from drug and alcohol abuse and abstain from premature sexual activity.
- Understand when to compete and when to cooperate.
- Neither bully nor be bullied.
- Build successful friendships and to become a leader when appropriate.
- Think critically and be creative problem finders and solvers.

In short, we want children to have social and emotional well-being. And this, of course, derives from SEL. Some parents think that schools should provide this instruction. Others believe it ought to take place at home. Wherever you think it ought to happen, clearly it isn't happening enough. Here's an example of what we mean:

In one ninth-grade class, a group of bored students calling themselves the "Six Sexy Sisters" decided to see if they could "bounce" some other girl from their school. They wondered if they could actually get her to transfer to another school without them getting caught. To add to the challenge, they chose their victim from among ordinary girls, not someone with an obvious handicap. They put 10 names into a hat and drew out a slip with Jessica C. on it. Then they began their online bullying campaign:

- When Jessica posted her Sweet 16 pictures online, they wrote anonymously "I'd rather cut off my arm than touch you, you're so ugly!"
- Another post: "Only cool girls wear the kind of pants you had on today, and you shouldn't wear them, because you are definitely not cool!"
- In an orchestrated attack, the girls signed onto a site, registering as Jennifer. Several members on the site were then attacked, and Jessica was blamed.
- Posing as a guy named Fred, they wrote on Jessica's Facebook page, "I hate u, everyone hates u … u should just die!"
- Using her boyfriend's name, they posted that he thought she was "just a slutty girl," and was through with her.

Jessica's school is in a state that has a mandated school policy: no tolerance for bullying. When Jessica complained to the principal, naming the six girls she suspected were bullying her, he asked each of the girls if she were guilty. Each denied participating, so the principal issued an announcement to all students that he would not tolerate bullying, thus fulfilling what he thought the mandate called for. The SSSs continued their vicious attacks with impunity. Now Jessica's family is suing the principal and district for nearly $2 million. They have a good chance of getting this money, which, of course, the district can ill afford. Would this have happened if this school had offered SEL instruction?

As reported in an online study, "Eighty percent of teens say they have read or spread gossip online; more than 50% say they have seen Web sites that made fun of their peers. Yet there seems to be a code of silence—what happens online stays online—leaving those who might help, in school and at home, in the dark".[6]

So how should society address social and emotional learning? One educational specialist answers this way: "SEL has gained traction in recent years, driven in part by concerns over school violence, bullying and teen suicide. But while prevention programs tend to focus on a single problem, the goal of SEL is grander: to instill a deep psychological intelligence that will help children regulate their emotions."[7] Teachers used to include SEL in their curricula, but not many do any more.

You will find few cross-disciplinary class projects, creativity exercises, or anti-bullying lessons these days in classrooms in the western world. The east is not that different.[8] Most educators are too busy imparting facts and academic skills, because their very jobs depend on how well their students succeed on high-stakes tests. These mostly multiple-choice tests primarily measure factual knowledge. Of course our children need to know these facts, but they must also experience and use SEL.

From newspaper headlines to parenting journals and forums, in parent-teacher groups and along the sidelines at school sporting events, SEL is becoming a hot topic. A national group, the Collaborative for Academic, Social and Emotional Learning (CASEL), has been formed, and about a third of the states in the United States have CASEL associations. Many teachers support and belong to these groups, as they are unhappy with the

6   beinggirl.com/, p. 1.
7   Kahn, 2013, p. 13.
8   Zhao, 2011.

current situation, too. Most did not go into the profession so they could drill children on facts. As one Seattle teacher puts it, "I am opposed to these tests because they narrow what education is supposed to be about. I think collaboration, imagination, and critical thinking skills are all left off these tests and can't be assessed by circling A, B, C, or D."[9] Many teachers would like to include SEL in the curriculum, but only if the instruction meets one of the Common Core State Standards. Because large numbers of parents have given up on changing school objectives, they are ready to pursue the goals of SEL in their own homes, on their own. Both groups want to learn how, but it looks like parents will have to take the lead.

Here is how one family researcher put it: "This is the actual crisis of parenting today—not whether we're breast feeding too little or 'helicoptering' too much, or feeding our kids the French way or teaching piano with Tiger ferocity, but whether we're abdicating our biggest responsibility—to make sure kids treat each other [and themselves] humanely."[10] This concern is not new. Eight years ago, Professor Jonathan Cohen, in a cogent article in the *Harvard Educational Review*, warned us about the looming problem in most U.S. classrooms:

> If federal and state policymakers and education colleges continue to ignore the importance of social/emotional competencies, I believe this amounts to a violation of human rights. Our children deserve better. This country deserves better."[11]

An Example of SEL

It might be said that there are two kinds of people in the world: "hedge-hogs" and "foxes." The hedgehog knows one big thing, the fox knows many things. Hedgehogs are in the majority. When they get a job with an organization, they stay there for many years and work their way up from within. They don't know much about how people outside their corporation do things, but they are experts within their business field.

Foxes, on the other hand, move from place to place. They know lots of ways to do things, but are seldom experts in any of them. In periods of

---

[9]   Zezima, 2013, p. 1.

[10] J. Weiss, 2013, p. A13.

[11] Cohen, 2006.

stability, hedgehogs are clearly the most valuable employees, but when things start changing quickly, the organization needs its flexible foxes.

Here's the rub. "A 2013 survey by a consulting firm of more than 500 executives revealed that hedgehogs 'have no clothes.' That is, a whopping 93% of respondents believed their company's long-term success depended on its ability to innovate, yet only 18% felt they had a competitive edge."[12] What lesson does this convey? Many countries in the world have too many hedgehogs and not enough foxes. How can we change this? Parents and professional educators must get better at delivering SEL to the children, so they can know when to be a reliable hedgehog, and when to be a creative fox!

Reciprocal Development and SEL

Another important aspect of SEL is the nature of the human brain. Cerebral structures develop according to a principle known as "reciprocal development." According to this process, changes in all animals are affected by the environment, which in turn is affected by changes in animals. Here are two examples:

- As trees grew taller, the necks of giraffes grew longer, and as taller giraffes ate leaves higher on a tree, leaves grew out of the top, making the tree taller yet.
- In the nineteenth century there were white and black moths. For some reason the bark of trees grew darker, and before long there were many more black moths than white.

The development of the human brain has operated in exactly this way. For example, some people are born with genes that give them a tendency toward being shy. As a result, their parents tend to be protective of them, which makes them even shyer. This has an effect on their hormonal balances, especially their estrogen, which in turn affects the direction of their brain development.

The opposite is true of children who are born with a tendency toward assertiveness and extraversion. Such children often have the confidence to contradict their parents and go against directions. Their parents, who also

---

[12]   Stanford U, 2013, p. 7.

are likely to have a tendency toward assertiveness, are likely to respond to the child's disobedience by being aggressive. This can make her be even more assertive, and because of the hormonal secretions that go along with this behavior, her brain is affected.

Another example of reciprocal development has to do with reading ability. Some children are born with a disability for reading; they may even be dyslexic. Others have a genetic makeup that favors reading ability. One study found that the number of new words learned by the first group in one year is equal to the number of new words learned by the second group in two days! It is likely that the number of words a person has in her vocabulary is highly related to her ability for social and emotional learning. After all, if you don't have the words for new concept, you are unlikely to learn it. Once again, we see the interdependence of academic learning with SEL. Too much emphasis on AL hurts learning of both types.

A Brief History of the SEL Movement

The birth of SEL as a field and movement can be tied to the research of Howard Gardner on multiple intelligences. His work helped us understand that there are several kinds of "smart." Beyond reading, writing, and math skills are social/emotional "intelligences" that are less test-friendly, but equally essential. Gardner identified eight types of intelligence and speculates that there may be more. Building on Gardner's work, Daniel Goleman[13] coined the term "emotional intelligence" to describe the ways in which we humans make sense of and act in the social world. Of course this is a reconsideration of what philosophers have been saying for ages. It involves a new look at the core values espoused by many of the world's major religions, such as "the Golden Rule." Goleman and others created an organization to move this work forward. The Collaborative for Academic, Social and Emotional Learning has become an important resource for educators, parents, and civic leaders who want to teach children SEL.

CASEL defines SEL as "developing the ability to recognize and manage emotions, develop caring and concern for others, make responsible decisions, establish positive relationships, and handle challenging situations effectively."[14]

---

[13]   Goleman, 1996.
[14]   Personal communication, Roger Weissberg, CASEL, Nov. 2015.

Research and evaluation studies that describe the impact of effective SEL programs, summarized by CASEL, suggest that these programs help children have:

- A deeper sense of connection to school.
- Improved skills for setting goals.
- Greater capacity to solve problems.
- Better self-discipline.
- Finer character and responsible values.

Several studies have also shown that SEL helps to improve students' academic success. CASEL has identified five basic social/emotional abilities. Let's take a brief look at how they appear in the life of a child.

- *Self-awareness.* As children develop they begin to recognize the emotions of others (the new parent's excitement in the hospital nursery, exhaustion from lack of sleep, and pride in the toddler's first steps). They also learn to recognize and then find words for their own emotions—first the simple ones (like happiness, sadness, and fear) and then the more complex ones (like disappointment, pride, worry, and anticipation). Along the way, they are learning how to manage their emotional world. They ask for help, stay silent in the face of fear, and talk excitedly about some new accomplishment. The ability to recognize and manage emotions is the first step in successful social living.
- *Self-management.* All children face hard times—although some must deal with intense challenges like homelessness, poverty, abuse, or other traumas that others fortunately avoid. Handling challenging situations effectively is one key to healthy development. Researchers have called this resilience, courage, and hopefulness. Handling difficult situations effectively gives a boost to the other four SEL skills. In fact, they all depend on each other for a person's ideal development.
- *Social awareness.* Infants express concern and caring long before they have speech—when they offer a toy or snack, or even cry at the sight of others crying. For most children, this ability expands to include broader and broader sets of people, from caregiver to play group to schoolmates. For some children, the circle of care and concern stays closed—perhaps because they have a hard time balancing the needs of others, or because

their history of hurt does not allow them to reach out (more on this in the next chapter). In both cases, social success requires the ability to express and then act on feelings. Children who are leaders usually have these twin abilities: they care about others and they can express that concern. Children who are isolated and lonely usually do not have these abilities, or they are unable to use them well.

- *Responsible decision-making.* Successful children, like successful adults, usually make responsible decisions. They make responsible decisions when they find and keep positive friends at school, take care of their health in a world that pushes substance abuse, and work hard at school and home.

- *Relationship skills.* We are all in relationships—but not all of them are positive. Positive relationships set limits that are caring and loving, and involve listening as much as talking. In positive relationships, children ask adults for help and see what happens next. They test limits and evaluate how others react to their misbehavior. The essence of a good relationship is *validation*—when an intimate friend or partner relates to your experience by acknowledging a confidence from you and then sharing a similar one (more on this magical process in the next chapter).

Parent–Teacher Alliances Need Support

As for parents, the answer is simple: parents (and grandparents) are a child's first teachers. There is truth in the adage, "Only parents and grand-parents can truly raise a child, because they are the only ones for whom that child's success is vital." These six people have a special love for and intimacy with their offspring. They care about them when fever comes at two in the morning, as much as when the first words come in the afternoon.

Teachers spend the most productive part of most weekdays observing what the child needs, how she communicates those needs, and how she responds to the needs of others. Parents and teachers often have special, one-on-one time with children—this provides crucial chances to teach social/emotional skills. And perhaps most importantly, a parent or a teacher can serve as a model for what it means to be a successful human being. Collaborations between the two are obviously superior to the independent actions of either one.

Using our Strategies to Teach SEL

Our book recommends strategies you can use to help children develop and strengthen humane values and skills in their own lives. It offers easy-to-follow exercises that include:

- Clear instructions for teaching the SEL strategy.
- The age group for whom the strategy was designed (plus recommended alterations for its use with the other age group).
- The goal(s) sought.
- Descriptions of materials you may need to implement the strategy.
- Suggested scripts you might say or paraphrase to instruct your child.

We hope that teachers, coaches, and counselors will use these strategies, but in this book we speak primarily to parents, as we assume that the professionals can easily adapt our strategies for classroom, homework, or therapeutic use.

Learning how to use these strategies and employing them need not take an inordinate amount of your time. Our strategies can be adapted easily to your children's ability levels, from ages 6 to 15. With each of these activities, we include specific exemplars for younger and older children, which you can then adapt as you see fit. You will probably want help from others with this vital task, and in Chapter 13 we suggest where and how you can get it. In the last chapter, we try to anticipate the future of the SEL movement, including new techniques that involve electronic devices and social networks. And finally, on our website (www.wiley.com/go/daceywellbeing), we provide ancillary materials and sources. We applaud you for caring enough to read this book, and sincerely hope we have provided you with everything you will need to be highly successful in this most important goal.

Part I

Self-awareness

2

Building Character

It takes real character to keep working even harder once you're there. When you read about an athlete or team that wins over and over and over, remind yourself, "More than ability, they have character."[1]

According to this view, character means being a winner. It's about sticktuitiveness, competitiveness, and grit. That's what many people think, anyway.

We disagree. Character is about many things, including the ability to be a good loser. It's knowing what you believe, but also about being willing to say you're wrong. It's standing up for the positions you have faith in, but also about being willing to re-examine your values, especially in the face of contrary information. In fact, these terms—virtue, excellence, goodness, moral righteousness, character—are pretty much synonymous.

We also believe that the most important virtue is being "right-sized," because without it, you cannot be a person of character. Psychologist Carl

---

[1] John Wooden, quoted in Dweck, 2006, p. 67.

Your Child's Social and Emotional Well-Being: A Complete Guide for Parents and Those Who Help Them, First Edition. John S. Dacey, Lisa B. Fiore, and Steven Brion-Meisels.
© 2016 John Wiley & Sons, Ltd. Published 2016 by John Wiley & Sons, Ltd.
Companion website: www.wiley.com/go/daceywellbeing

Rogers offers a good way to look at what right-sized means.[2] He says that everyone has two images of themselves:

- Their *ideal self*, which comprises all the traits they would like to believe they possess;
- Their *real self*, which comprises all the traits they actually have.

Rogers's insight was that the greater the distance between to the two, the greater the inner conflict the person suffers. There is a "war" being carried out in the psyche of the conflicted which makes it harder for them to be virtuous. They lack self-knowledge, and therefore the power they need, to be all they can be. Rogers calls such a person "self-actualized."

Diagrammatically, a healthy psyche looks

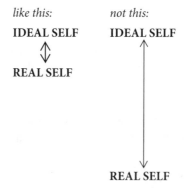

Rogers suggested that there exist three possible remedies:

- Lower one's ideal expectations to a more reasonable level.
- Raise one's real efforts to succeed to a more reasonable level.
- And (usually) both.

When the two self-images are closely aligned, people are said to be "right-sized." Their knowledge of themselves matches real-world objectivity. As William Shakespeare put it in *Hamlet*, "To thine own self be true, and it must follow, as the night the day, thou canst not then be false to any man." Knowing and showing yourself accurately is the essential first step in becoming a person of character.

[2]   Rogers, Lyon, and Tausch, 2013.

Are today's youth learning to become virtuous? Here's what *New York Times* editorialist David Brooks, who also teaches a course on character at Yale, has to say:

> "When it comes to character and virtue, these young people have been left on their own. Today's go-getter parents and today's educational institutions work frantically to cultivate neural synapses, to foster good study skills, to promote musical talents. We spend huge amounts of money on safety equipment and sports coaching. We sermonize about the evils of drunk driving. We expend enormous energy guiding and regulating their lives. But when it comes to character and virtue, the most mysterious area of all, suddenly the laissez-faire ethic rules: You're on your own, Jack and Jill; go figure out what is true and just for yourselves.[3]

Forming Character: Awareness and Openness

Knowing yourself and revealing that self judiciously to others are crucial to character-building. We are fortunate to have the research of Joseph Luft and Harry Ingham. Their work generated the "Johari Window."[4]

The Johari Window

The Johari Window is a technique for charting a person's awareness of himself and his openness to others. Let's suppose there are four characteristics that are true of you. You are:

1. A man.
2. Can't stand the "chatter" of women.
3. Someone who talks too much.
4. An alcoholic.

Of these four traits,

1. Everyone knows the first.
2. Only you know the second (you were trained that way by your mother, who was herself a misogynist), and you are ashamed of it.

---

[3] Brooks, 2006.
[4] Adapted from Human Resourcefulness, 2014.

3. You are unaware that most of your friends and family agree on the third.
4. Neither you nor your friends and family have realized yet that you have become dependent on alcohol.

Suppose all the things that are true of you were equally divided between these four types of self-awareness, 25 percent in each category, According to the Johari Window system, it would graphically look like this.

A Johari Window with awareness divided equally among the four conditions

Known to All	Known Only to Self
Known Only to Others	Hidden from All

However, the degree to which we know ourselves (awareness) and share ourselves with others (disclosure) is a measure of mental health. "You're only as sick as your secrets," according to the Alcoholics Anonymous *Big Book*.[5] That is, the more open you are with yourself and others, the less time you have to spend, unconsciously, defending yourself from the truth.

Sigmund Freud's explanation of personality[6] depended heavily on self-knowledge and public revelation. He held that the most powerful enemies of both are "defense mechanisms." These are unconscious attempts to suppress unpleasant or unacceptable truths *about one's self, from one's self*. The literature describes almost 50 different kinds, such as:

*   *Compensation*: Attempting to make up for an unconsciously perceived inadequacy by excelling at something else (e.g., if unable to be a superior athlete, a person becomes a sports writer).
*   *Regression*: Reverting to behaviors that were previously successful when current behavior is unsuccessful (e.g., when becoming frustrated with a problem, act childishly or cry about it).
*   *Compartmentalization*: Having two mutually incompatible beliefs at the same time (e.g., "I am above average in my schoolwork," and "Most of my classmates are a lot smarter than me").

---

5   Alcoholics Anonymous, 2014.
6   Freud Psychoanalysis, 2014.

Let's take an SEL example. Freud firmly believed that people are most motivated to be creative when they cannot directly fulfill their sexual needs (see Chapter 11). Hence he held that sublimation (when unable to fulfill one's sex drives, making up for it by being artistic) is the primary cause of creativity. So firmly did he believe this that after the age of 40, he refrained from sexual intercourse with his wife in order to improve his imaginative mind!

There are two serious problems with the use of defense mechanisms. They use up a lot of psychic energy, and they always distort the truth. As such they are to be avoided whenever possible. A person who does so would have a Johari Window like this:

The ideal Johari Window

Known to All	Known Only to Self
Known Only to Others	Hidden from All

Why is the "known to all" pane so large, and the other three panes commensurately smaller? Luft and Ingham[7] argue (in agreement with Freud) that psychologically healthy individuals are those who employ the fewest defense mechanisms. Therefore they are "known to self." In addition, because they have carefully examined their values, and have no shame about those values, they are "known to others," too. Aspects of their personalities which are "hidden from all" are few.

Although, in this book, the strategies we recommend are primarily for use by one parent and one child, you might want to look into whole programs designed for classrooms to enhance character formation. These include:

- The Caring School Community
- Promoting Alternative Thinking Strategies (PATHS)
- Positive Action
- The Responsive Classroom Approach
- Second Step
- Tribes Learning Communities
- RULER

[7] Human Resourcefulness, 2014.

- 6 Seconds
- MindUp
- Resolving Conflict Creatively
- 4 Rs (Reading, Writing, Respect, and Resolution)[8]

ACTIVITY

Behind the Classroom Door

Target age: 6 to 10

Goal: To become more aware of one's true nature, and reveal it honestly to another

Materials needed: None

Script: Imagine that you are in a classroom, behind an open door. A small group of your friends are standing out in the hallway. You can hear them, but they don't know you're there. One of them says, "I really like [your child's name] because he's …" What is that person probably saying? Does it make you feel good to know they think that about you?

Now suppose another child says, "Well, there is one thing I don't like about him and [your child's name]: he's …" What do you think that person is probably saying about you? Does it hurt your feelings to hear that? [Repeat this same sequence of these two questions two more times.] How would you feel if everyone knew about the good things those friends were saying about you? How would you feel if everyone knew the bad things they said? Do you think it's good for people to know everything about you, even if some of those things hurt your feelings?

Adaptation for older children: Pursue these questions more fully with older children. Explore the idea of being "right-sized," and that having others know both good and bad things about them helps to develop character.

---

[8]   Rimm-Kaufman & Hulleman, 2015.

ACTIVITY

 2B

My Hero!

Target Age: 11 to 16
Goal: To help your child become clearer on the meaning of character
Materials needed: Pen, pencil, or your own electronic device
Script: A hero is someone you admire. You may not have met this person, but you think they are really special. This is someone you hope to grow up like. Can you tell me this person's name? If you don't have a hero now, let's spend a few minutes trying to think of one.

Now I want you to tell me about this person's traits. For example, is he or she:

- Smart or just of average intelligence?
- Handsome or beautiful?
- Married or single?
- Strong or weak?
- Rich or poor?
- Tall or short?
- Kind or mean?

Now, let's look over your answers and see what it tells us about you. Is this person like you? How is he or she different from you? Do you wish you were more like him or her? What can you do to be more like her or him?

Adaptation for older children: You can use more complex characteristics, such as leader/follower, insightful, etc. You can also push your child to be more specific about what he considers the traits of a person with character to be.

Building Character: Transcultural Experience

One of the most effective ways of building character, such as sensitivity to the needs of others and awareness of one's own prejudices, is to spend time in a culture quite different from your own. Here is a story about someone who did that.

My Mexican Childhood[9]

By Elizabeth Goizueta, art curator and professor, Boston College

When I was seven, my father, a sculptor and professor, moved our family from Athens, Georgia in the U.S. (where he taught at the University) to Cuernavaca, Mexico. He had been awarded a grant to study the art that flourished there due to the financial boost of the 1968 Olympics. Our parents thought this would be an excellent opportunity for us to have a cultural experience. Everything was different, or so it seemed. I remember pledging allegiance to the Mexican flag every morning in our Mexican school. Translated from Spanish, it goes like this:

> *"Mexican flag, legacy from our heroes, symbol of the unity of our parents and our brothers:*
> *We promise you to be always loyal to the principles of freedom and justice that makes this an independent, human and generous nation, to which we dedicate our existence."*

I was so young, I felt no allegiances to any country, and dutifully repeated the words daily. Of greater concern was, could I quickly learn to speak Spanish and fit in, as I was attending a school with only Mexican children? On the first day of class, to my dismay, I also discovered that they already wrote in cursive, and I had only learned to print! However, at home we were surrounded by Mexican household helpers, including a 16-year-old daughter who dealt with the massive load of laundry, and with her help I quickly learned the basics. We lived near some beautiful Aztec ruins. …

Also, we were immersed in Mexican art and artists, as my father was studying the Mexican muralist painters Diego Rivera, David Álfaro Siqueiros, and José Clemente Orozco. Aztec influences permeated our house and my father's work.

After my older brother was almost kidnapped, and the 1968 Mexican student protests demanding greater democracy resulted in a student massacre, my parents decided not to finish out the year. It was time to leave Mexico. When we got back to the U.S., I was shocked to discover how terrified my parents had really felt, living in this country that they so deeply admired and respected. We were targeted as "gringos" (derived from "green grows," a term that developed during the Mexican–American war). Gringos were seen as rich, but too naïve to navigate the not-too-subtle layers of corruption.

---

[9]   Story reproduced by kind permission of Elizabeth Goizueta.

Nevertheless, I think it had a great benefit, which resulted in this resolute value: never trust what someone tells you. Check things out for yourself! That is not to say you should be hyper-suspicious. However, as the Russians say, "Trust but verify," especially when it comes to information about another culture. It is a value I have tried to teach my three children, not by lecturing, but through multicultural experiences.

ACTIVITY

Transcultural Insight

Target age: 11 to 15

Goal: To clarify your child's values through exposure to a different culture

Materials needed: Your own electronic device, connected to the Web

Script: If you could visit another country today, what would it be? Okay, let's go online and find out what we can about the country. We'll need to find the answers to these questions first:

- What is the most popular food in this country? Why you think that is?
- How is the country governed? Dictator? Elected representatives? Military junta?
- How does the country make most of its money? Agriculture? Manufacture? Tourism?
- Who are the most famous people in this country, and what jobs do they have?
- What are the most important geological features of this country? Surrounded by water? Flatland? Hot?
- What sport is most popular in this country? Skiing? Soccer? Diving?
- What questions can you think of that would help you to understand this country better?

Look over your answers to these questions. How would living in this country make you a different person? Do you think you would like yourself better or less well if you lived there?

Adaptation for younger children: You will need to help your child find the answers. You will also need to assist him to figure out how he would be different.

Building Character: Humility

The word "humility" is much misunderstood. It is often taken to mean having low self-esteem or being self-effacing. The opposite of the boastful fellow, some think the humble individual regards himself as having little worth. Once again we turn to essayist David Brooks to set the picture straight:

> the humble person has an accurate view of himself. He can acknowledge his mistakes. He has low self-focus. He is aware of his place in the grand scheme of things and is sensitive to larger and possibly higher forces. Humility is not modesty, either … The modest person has an adequate view of himself, but may still think about himself all the time. Humility is better seen as the opposite of narcissism. The narcissist has a damaged sense of self and is consequently self-centered, reacting in defensive ways to ego threat. The humble person has an accurate and durable sense of self and can see the relationship between the self and the larger world.[10]

Brooks points to "people who exemplify successful lives of self-restraint and self-distrust."[11] By self-restraint he means refraining from the need to brag about your own accomplishments, and by self-distrust he means having a healthy suspicion that you are biased toward yourself. That is, you are "right-sized."

We are reminded of the story of the recovering alcoholic on his way to address a meeting of his fellows. Asked what his topic would be, he replied, "Humility, but only if there are at least 100 at the meeting. Otherwise I can't be bothered." He is making a joke about being "right-sized."

ACTIVITY

Humility Times

Target age: 11 to 15
Goal: To develop greater clarity on the meaning of humility
Materials needed: Pencil and paper, or your own electronic device
Script: It isn't always easy to know when someone is being humble (right-sized). It might be fun to know what our neighbors think

---

[10]   Brooks, 2011, p. 31.
[11]   Coscarelli, 2013, p. 1.

it means. How about if you write one issue of a neighborhood newspaper that only reports on the activities of individuals who demonstrate being humble? You would have to interview the neighbors, asking them to give you examples of the actions of people they know who would qualify. You could type it up, it out, and distribute it to everyone on your street. I think they would all be happy that you did it, and you would have several good examples of what humility actually means.

Adaptation for younger children: You could help your child to do this activity just within your family.

ACTIVITY

The Prideful Pig

Target age: 6 to 10

Goal: This strategy for teaching humility was designed by Katherine Hatter. She says, "Humility is putting others first and elevating others before yourself; pride is flaunting the self and putting yourself first."[12]

Materials needed: Paper and drawing mediums (crayons, markers, or paint)

Script: I'm going to ask you to draw a picture of two pigs. The proud pig might have a big head, a little heart an an upturned snout, because he doesn't care about anyone but himself. The humble pig might have a big heart, big ears (for hearing about others' needs) and long legs with big muscles for helping others. What other ways can you show that the second pig is right-sized?

Adaptation for older children: For this age group, drawing two human figures would be more complex, but would also allow for more subtle differences between the prideful and the humble character.

---

[12] Hatter, 2014.

ACTIVITY

Books-on-Humility Scavenger Hunt

Target age: 11 to 16

Goal: To hone your child's definition of humility

Materials needed: Access to a library or online bookseller

Script: I think that humility is a characteristic that everybody needs to develop. One of the best ways to do that is to read what experts have to say. Therefore, there is going to be a prize for you if you can find 10 sources on the subject. You can look online, such as searching Amazon.com, and you can also look in the library. When we have descriptions of 10 books, we will select one of them and read it together. I want to do this because I would like both both of us to increase our level of humility. Are you willing to undertake this quest? To get you started, let me tell you the name of one book that I would recommend: *Humility: True Greatness*, by C.J. Mahaney and Joshua Harris. See if you can find a description of it and nine other books. Good luck!

Adaptation for younger children: For them, you'll probably have to assist with the search, and you will need to choose children's books, of course. Perhaps the prize should be awarded for five finds rather than 10.

ACTIVITY

Sunday Afternoon at the Soup Kitchen

Target age: 6 to 15

Goal: To deepen your child's awareness of himself through contact with those who are different

Materials needed: Access to a soup kitchen

Script: I have made plans to volunteer at a nearby place that serves lunch to homeless people. I would love it if you'd come along with me. They will tell us everything we need to know when we get there. Afterwards, we can discuss the experience and see what each of us has learned. Are you game?

Building Character: Modeling

One way to teach your child humility is to model telling the truth. That is what David McCullough, Jr., did in his address to the graduating class of Wellesley High School recently. He said,

> You are not special. You are not exceptional.
> Contrary to what your soccer trophy suggests, your glowing seventh grade report card, despite every assurance of a certain corpulent purple dinosaur, that nice Mister Rogers and your batty Aunt Sylvia, no matter how often your maternal caped crusader has swooped in to save you … you're nothing special.

We do not mean to imply that your child's ego needs battering. And it is true that some children are indeed special, in any of a number of ways. Overall, however, the great majority of children fit into the average range. Trying to convince them otherwise is to make them "wrong-sized," and that does nobody any good. Probably the best way to teach humility is to model what it means.

My Role-modeling Parents[13]
By Allyson Shumur, recent Boston College graduate and psychiatric nursing assistant at U. Penn. Hospital

Children can definitely tell when their parents are truly humble. For example, both of my parents have a lot to be proud of. They were varsity athletes at Michigan State U., my mother as a member of a Big 10 Championship swim team, my father as co-captain of the 1988 Rose Bowl Championship team. As offensive coach for the Philadelphia Eagles, my father regularly works 16-hour days. However, he doesn't ask a single thing of us kids except that we get good grades and get our "business" done. My mother is a stay-at-home mom who might as well have a full time job, dealing with all of our activities. At 22, I am the eldest, I have a 21-year-old sister, an 18-year-old brother, and my youngest sister is 12. As you can imagine, we are a handful.

Although my parents have a lot of work to do, you would never know it. They do not brag or complain about how hard they work. They simply do it with humility. They believe that just as you cannot really impose religion on anyone, children will develop their own ideals simply by observing their parents.

---

[13] Reproduced by kind permission of Allyson Shumur.

Mom and Dad also have made sure to expose us children to the arts and literature. This way they encourage our individual creativity. When we succeed, they remind us that although it is the result of our hard work, we should also be grateful for the gifts we have been given.

Finally, they've made sure we know that many people survive with much less than we have. We are very fortunate. I am so appreciative that my parents had such expectations for me and my siblings, and that gradually we have come to accept them for ourselves.

ACTIVITY

Modeling Humility

Target age: 11 to 15

Goal: To improve your ability to model humility for your children

Materials needed: None

Script: Humility is being who you really are, neither too big nor too small for your britches. Exactly what do I mean by that? In the next week, at least once each day, I'm going to try to be a model of humility. Every time that you think I am speaking or acting in a humble way, I would like you to write down a description of what happened. To make sure that you get at least one example every day, you are allowed to ask one daily question. If you think my answer demonstrates humility, write down that example. If you can think of an example every day for one week, I'm going to give you a gift to show my appreciation for your paying attention. I don't want to say what it is right now, but you can be sure that you're going to like it.

Adaptation for younger children: Younger children may have a difficult time spotting humble behavior on their own. Each day, you may want to do something that demonstrates humility, and then ask your child what he thinks was right-sized about it.

Building Character: Courage

Defining courage can be tricky. An action which may be courageous for one person may not be so for another. For a young recruit to charge an enemy position may be terrifying to him, whereas to the experienced soldier it may only be mildly frightening. To the deranged soldier whose mind has run amok, it may not take any courage at all, as he may not even know what he is doing. Like self-control, courage is only courage if something is hard to do.

Malala Yousafzai: "The Bravest Girl in the World"

Malala was a 12-year-old student attending a Pakistani school when she wrote a blog for the BBC. She supported the rights of girls to an education, even though the ruling Taliban had banned females from attending school. As Malala gained prominence for her writing, South African Bishop Desmond Tutu nominated her for the International Children's Peace Prize.

In October of 2012, a Taliban gunman boarded her school bus and shot her three times in the face. She was in a critical condition for days, but improved enough to continue her recovery and rehabilitation in England. The Taliban continued with their threats to kill her and her father, but she would not cease to speak out for her young sisters throughout southern Asia. On December 16, 2014, the day of an attack on a military school in Pakistan by the Taliban that claimed 141 lives, the great majority of them children, she said she was "heartbroken over this cowardly act."

Malala's bravery and activism for women's right to education has brought support from all over the world. A UN petition, "I am Malala," was born. The petition's focus was for all children worldwide to have the right to be educated in school by December 2015. The initiative led to the ratification of Pakistan's first Right to Education Bill. She has been recognized with over 30 distinguished honors and awards from many countries, including being the youngest winner ever of the Nobel Peace Prize in 2014.

ACTIVITY

 2|

Brave Kid

Target age: 6 to 10
Goal: To experience the rewards of being brave
Materials needed: Depends on the plan chosen
Script: *"The purpose of life is a life of purpose."*[14] What do you think this motto means? It is hard to live a life of purpose if you are saddled with phobias. Do you know what the word "phobia" means? Do you think you have any?

[Suppose your young child is frightened of dogs. Most children 6 to 10 years old are.] If you follow my instructions with bravery and determination, you will actually be able to handle a dog at the end of this exercise. What's that you say? "But I don't care about handling dogs!" This is not about dogs, it's about learning how to become more courageous. And that is one of the most important virtues you can ever attain.

I know you are more frightened of dogs because of an unfortunate incident when you were younger. Therefore it is going to take courage to get so you can actually pet a dog. Of course it is! How would you get enough bravery to reach this goal? Step by step.

When you have been able to persuade your child to try to achieve this goal, (or some other), the steps to achieve this objective need to go something like this:

A. Look at a picture of a dog.
B. Grasp a small toy dog.
C. Do the two together.
D. Watch a film about dogs.
E. Hold a stuffed dog.
F. Look at a dog in a cage.
G. Do the two together.
H. Touch a small dog with your fingertip.
I. Briefly rub your fingers in the dog's fur.
J. Pet the dog for one minute.
K. Pet a larger dog for one minute.

[14] Sonnenberg, 2014.

Set up a schedule for trying to achieve each of these subgoals, with an appropriate reinforcement for each success.

That's wonderful—I'm so proud of you! With each passing step, you showed a lot of courage. What does it feel like to be so brave? Where does courage come from? Do you have any other unreasonable fears, such as looking down from high places? Next week, would you like to try to tackle that problem?

Adaptation for older children: Choose a more difficult goal, such as giving a speech before an audience.

ACTIVITY

The Good Ones

Target age: 5 to 10

Goal: To help your child identify with the failures and the unflagging determination of real and imaginary heroes and heroines

Materials needed: Whatever book(s) you o r your child choose to read

Script: Because they usually possess excellent imaginations, children are often able to identify with stories about imaginary heroes and heroines. You should find it easy to locate biographies and historical fictions that are at an appropriate level for your child. As you read a story, occasionally ask your child one or more of these questions:

What do you think of the person in the story? Do you admire her?
Would you like to be like her?
Why do you think she is successful?
What could you do to be more like her?
How would your life be different if you were more like her?

Examples of heroes might be Paul Bunyan, Abraham Lincoln, Michael Jordan, George Washington, Superman, Moses, Jesus, Buddha, and Kermit the Frog. Examples of heroines might be Wonder Woman, Althea Gibson, the Blessed Virgin Mary, Wilma C, Joan of Arc, Oprah

Winfrey, Amelia Earhart, Pocahontas, and Helen Keller. Any children's librarian could suggest many more.

Adaptation for older children: Checking with your children's librarian will get you many suggestions for older children, too. They will be able to read the stories by themselves, and might like to write out the answers to the questions privately.

Building Character: Clear Values

Values clarification is a technique that helps people achieve conviction about what to do in life. Rather than telling a child what a principled position would be, it emphasizes personal discovery through discussions with others. Values can be likened to guidelines which give direction. When their guidelines are blurred or unclear, people usually have difficulty making decisions. Those who have clear values, such as a firm intention to be more creative, tend to be purposeful and enthusiastic.[15]

What does the term "values" actually mean? Valuing is composed of seven processes:

- *Prizing and cherishing.* If a value is truly a value to us, we have a sense of being glad about it.
- *Publicly affirming, when appropriate.* If we are really proud of a value we hold, we should be willing to let anyone else know that we feel that way.
- *Choosing from alternatives.* A value which we hold because we have no choice is no value at all.
- *Choosing after consideration of consequences.* Obviously, a snap judgment about the importance of something does not really indicate a deep value.
- *Choosing freely.* If we are being forced by someone else to take a particular position, it cannot be said to really be our own value. As the old adage goes, "When we have to do something, we are not sure we want to, and we're pretty sure we don't."
- *Acting.* A real value should be one on which we are willing to take action.
- *Acting with pattern, consistency, and repetition.* In the case of a true value, we should be willing not only to act but to act as part of our normal pattern. People can see this is the way we really feel about a particular issue because this is the way we regularly act about it.

[15]   Simons, 1995.

ACTIVITY

Who Am I?

Target age: 11 to 16
Goal: Help your child learn more about himself
Materials needed: The chart below, pencil and paper or your own electronic device

Activity Rating Scale

Activity type	Example of activity	Your own example	Rating
Help your town	Clean up litter along the riverbank		
Work in a group	Volunteer at a soup kitchen		
Organize a group	Start your own class newspaper		
Work under high stress	Produce a newspaper in two days		
Work by yourself	Write a story		
Make yourself feel better	Eat ice cream		
Pay for a change in the way you look	Get a different kind of haircut		
Get change in the way you look for free	Lose weight		
Improve your mind	Take an online course		
Become more spiritual	Study Buddhism		
Become a calmer person	Take a course in yoga		

Script: Please read over this activity scale. Now, in the third column for each of these activities, write down your own example of how you would carry out the activity. Put a number that reflects how much you like that activity. Put a 1 if you don't care for it much, put a 2 if you somewhat like it, and a 3 if you like it a lot.

Now let's look at the activities to which you assigned a 3, the ones you like the most. What do they have in common? What else can you say about a person who gave the highest rating to these activities? What does all this tell us about you?

Adaptation for younger children: Because the strategy is somewhat abstract, younger children usually have a difficult time with it. There's no harm in trying to adjust it so that it makes sense to your younger children, however.

ACTIVITY

What Our Family Stands For

Target age: 11 to 16
Goal: Recognize and adopt family values (your values)
Materials needed: None
Script: You have probably heard your (mother/father) and me talk about what we think is right. Can you remember something we said? Yes, that's true. How about something else? [Continue this for about five minutes, allowing for time to think.] Okay, that's a great list. I would say you were paying attention!

Now I'd like you to tell me one idea with which you agree. Why do you think that's the right way to think? Any others? Why?

Okay, can you tell me one of our values you've heard with which you don't agree. Why not? Don't be afraid to differ with us—I really want to know what you think.

How do you think we decide on our values? Why is that important? Can you give me an example of a time when you acted on one of your values, when that was hard to do?

Adaptation for children: You will have to be much more directive with younger children. For example, you will probably have to suggest a specific value, stated appropriately. Nevertheless. we find that children in the 6- to 10-year age group can talk about their values, and really need to!

Undesirable Character Traits

As important as it is to help your child build character, it is also useful to lead him to avoid false or destructive influences. Probably the most impactful of these is friends.

ACTIVITY

Birds of a Feather

Target age: 6 to 10

Goal: To identify bad influences among your child's friends, by deciding on traits that make them bad influences

Materials: None

Script: I would like you to think about all the boys (or girls) in your class. Name your three best friends. Okay, now I want you to think about the others. Are there any you don't want to be friends with? Now, think about which of those kids you want to avoid because you think they are bad for you. Do you believe that other kids can make you be bad? How? Choose just one and tell me why you think he could have a bad effect on you. Any others?

Adaptation for older children: The main difference is terminology. With older kids, you can use words like destructive and influence.

ACTIVITY

A Bad Place to Be

Target age: 11 to 16

Goal: To identify places and situations that may have a negative impact on your child's character

Materials: Internet connection; computer

Script: The newspapers are full of stories about kids getting into trouble on the Internet. There are people there pretending to be another kid your age. They do this so they can talk you into behavior you normally wouldn't think of doing. Sometimes it's sexual, sometimes it's criminal. These people are amazingly good at convincing you that wrong is right. Most kids who have gotten into trouble thought they were doing nothing wrong.

Another way the Internet can corrupt your character is through bullying. This usually is caused by people who say really mean things without revealing their own identity. A good example is Ask.fm, a website where people can ask and answer questions anonymously. Unfortunately, it has developed as a hostile environment where a lot of cyberbullying occurs. Let's go to that site and see what we can learn about its dangers.

It is a good idea to situate the family computer in a common area so your child knows you might look over his shoulder unexpectedly. You also will need to learn how to use all of the security and privacy settings on Internet browsers and social media sites. Be sure to check the browser history and the cookies on the computer to detect any suspicious sites. Many free resources are available to you to keep your kids safe online!

Adaptation for younger children: Children who are 6 to 10 should probably not have access to the Internet, but they are not too young to begin teaching them Internet safety.

And now for one more overall activity.

ACTIVITY

 2O

Attaboy!!

Target age: 6 to 10
Goal: Make clear to your child what character means
Materials needed: None
Script: We've talked a lot about what character means, but it has to be more than just talk. To be a person of character, you also have to "walk the walk." By that, I mean it matters that you don't just believe in our family's values, you also have to act on them.

Therefore, for the next week, I am going to fill out this chart by putting a 1, a 2, or a 3 in a box for each day of the week, each time I see you acting with virtue. That means you SHOW that you have character by what you do in everyday life. After I enter a score, in the next box I will write a note about what you did to earn that score. There is no limit to your total score each day.

At the end of one week, if your total score is between 14 and 21, you will receive a present of [X]. If your total score is between 22 and 35, you will receive a present of [Y]. If your total score is more than 36, you will receive a present of [Z]. The reason we are doing this activity is to make it clearer to you what character means. Therefor we will discuss how you did, and whether you would like to do this again for another week.

You will have to decide what constitutes appropriate gifts. They shouldn't be too extravagant, but should be capable of producing serious effort on the part of your child. Also, you should be a bit generous with your scoring the first week, and a little tougher if you decide to continue this practice. With children this age, you may want to remind them what actions constitute character (being kind to a troublesome sibling, helping with a household chore without being asked, etc.).

You may feel that this strategy involves bribery. However, the theory is that "Virtue becomes its own reward." Psychologists call this "moving from extrinsic to intrinsic motivation." The idea is to reward behaviors that are not natural to the child, with the goal of having them become natural. That is, virtuous behavior becomes habitual because the child feels better about himself when he does them, and the extrinsic reward is gradually withdrawn. We think you may be surprised at how well this works,

Adaptation for older children: You will not need to give as much explicit direction to older children. In fact, giving vague instructions promotes their well-being by forcing them to think about the meaning of character, and how to demonstrate that one has it.

Leo Rosten, author of *The Joys of Yiddish*, says that "mensch" is "someone to admire and emulate, someone of noble character. The key to being 'a real mensch' is nothing less than character..."[16] So go raise a mensch!

[16] Kawasaki, 2015, p. 1.

3

Practicing Mindfulness

Psychologist Ellen Langer says the *unmindful* person is one who "is often in error, but seldom in doubt."[1] This is because that individual has come to believe most of the information she has is unquestionably true, and therefore she no longer needs to pay it any mind. The essence of mindfulness, however, is paying attention.

The transformation brought about by mindfulness

> comes directly out of our ability to take a larger perspective, to realize that we are bigger than who we think we are. It comes directly out of recognizing and inhabiting the full dimensionality of our being, of being who and what we actually are. It turns out that these innate internal resources—which we can discover for ourselves and draw upon—all rest on that awareness."[2]

You are reading these words, so you have opened your mind to the possibility of change—as a parent, grandparent, or professional who is interested in learning more about promoting and sustaining SEL. The desire to find balance in your life is perhaps felt more acutely now than ever before. Your mind is often buzzing with the energy required to stay on top of the myriad

---

[1] Langer, December 5, 2014.
[2] Kabat-Zinn, 2013, p. xxvii.

Your Child's Social and Emotional Well-Being: A Complete Guide for Parents and Those Who Help Them, First Edition. John S. Dacey, Lisa B. Fiore, and Steven Brion-Meisels.
© 2016 John Wiley & Sons, Ltd. Published 2016 by John Wiley & Sons, Ltd.
Companion website: www.wiley.com/go/daceywellbeing

of activities, appointments, homework assistance, meals to prepare—all the tasks you perform for family, friends, and in the workplace. Mental fatigue is quite common, as is the physical exhaustion that accompanies all of the work that caregiving demands.

You have likely heard or read about mindfulness. While the concept is not new, recent research has improved our understanding of the contemplative practices associated with it, such as meditation.[3] For well over 5,000 years, cultures and societies have taught and studied mindful practices.

Dr. Jon Kabat-Zinn is the founder of the Stress Reduction Clinic at the University of Massachusetts Medical Center and creator of the Mindfulness-based Stress Reduction program (MBSR). He is the author of several books that describe mindfulness practices and make explicit the connections between body and mind, mental processes and science. Kabat-Zinn's book, *Full Catastrophe Living*,[4] has become for many the classic text that describes mindfulness and makes it accessible to all readers through its wise, simple, and validating content. He states that:

> Mindfulness is a skill that can be developed through practice, just like any other skill. You could also think of it as a muscle. The muscle of mindfulness grows both stronger and more supple and flexible as you use it. And like a muscle, it grows best when working with a certain amount of resistance to challenge it and thereby help it become stronger.[5]

Another individual who is highly regarded in the field, particularly with respect to meditation, is Sharon Salzberg. She emphasizes mindfulness as a choice—we may choose to wake up and notice the things that we often miss or ignore because we so often function on autopilot.[6] Salzberg also emphasizes the concept of "loving kindness," which involves forgiving and being kind to others, but also, and equally important, to ourselves. In her book, *Real Happiness*, she says, "something has kicked open the door for you, and you're ready to embrace change. It isn't enough to appreciate change from afar, or only in the abstract, or as something that can happen to other

[3]   One example is the collaborative effort of Oprah Winfrey and Deepak Chopra, who have joined forces to promote meditation: see the following website: https://chopracenter meditation.com
[4]   Kabat-Zinn, 1990/2013.
[5]   Kabat-Zinn, 1990/2013, p. xxxiii.
[6]   Salzberg, 2011.

people but not to you. We need to create change for ourselves, in a workable way, as part of our everyday lives."[7]

The activities that follow are all designed to increase your child's sense of present awareness.

Activities that Foster Awareness

ACTIVITY

Just Breathe ...

Target age: 11 to 15
Goal: To substantially increase your child's awareness of her physical responses
Materials needed: None
Script: Let's begin with a few moments to just ... breathe. The wonderful thing about breathing is that it happens automatically—you often don't even notice it—and it is a natural connection between your body and your mind. When you take time to focus on your breath, you begin to notice the present moment in a clear, calm, and focused way.

1. Find a comfortable position. You may feel relaxed sitting in a chair or lying flat on the floor. Take a moment to get comfortable—find a position that feels good to you. Close your eyes.
2. Observe where you are right now—notice where your body is touching the chair [or the floor]. Pay attention to your hands in your lap [or by your sides on the floor]. As you rest comfortably, notice what you're feeling in your body. Start with your toes and work your way up your legs, past your knees and thighs, past your hips, stomach, and back, along your arms, across your shoulders, up the back of your neck and to the top of your head. Observe the muscles in your face, and just ... Breathe.

---

[7]   Salzberg, 2013.

3. Now take a deep breath—through your nose or through your mouth—and then exhale slowly through your nose or mouth, noticing the sensation as the air enters and leaves your body. Notice the air as it enters your nose/mouth—is it cool? Warm? Where do you feel the air? Do you feel it inside your nostrils? On the back of your throat? Notice your stomach rising and falling with your breaths. You might place one or both hands on your tummy to feel it rise and fall with each breath.

4. As you pay attention to the in and out breath, you might notice thoughts entering your mind. You might notice feelings in parts of your body. What are you thinking or feeling? Now bring your attention back to your breath. Continue the breathing for approximately 3 minutes.

Adaptation for younger children: To help focus your child's attention on her breathing, say,

Breathe in one, breathe out one; Breathe in two, breathe out two; Breathe in three, breathe out three; Breathe in four, breathe out four,

until you reach a count of ten. You can also have your child place her hands on her thighs if sitting and on her tummy if lying down, and when you say Breathe in one, she presses her left pinky finger gently into her thigh or tummy. When you say Breathe in two, she presses her left ring finger gently into her thigh or tummy, and so on.

ACTIVITY

Mindful Eating

Target age: 11 to 15

Goal: To improve your child's awareness of the present moment

Materials needed: You may choose to use small, individual foil-wrapped chocolates, like Hershey's Kisses or Dove chocolate Promises (LF's preference!), or you may use fruit, such as a few raisins or an orange.

Script: Sit with your hands comfortably in your lap, and notice your breath for a few moments. Now concentrate on *the piece of chocolate*[8] in your hands or notice the color of the wrapper [or peel] and its size and how it feels as you run your fingers gently over its surface. Observe any bumps or creases. Bring the *piece of chocolate* to your nose and smell it. What do you like about the aroma? You may find that your thoughts wander, and if that happens simply notice them and let them go, then return your attention to your breathing.

When you are ready, place your fingers on the *piece of chocolate* and notice how it feels—soft, solid, bumpy? Using a fingertip or fingernail, gently lift an edge of the wrapper [peel] on the *piece of chocolate*, and break off a piece of *the chocolate*. What does it feel like? Bring your finger to your nose and become aware of the thoughts and feelings that come into your mind.

Now remove the wrapper [or peel] slowly, little by little, and when it is all off hold the *piece of chocolate* in your hand, noticing the lines and markings on it, making it unique and wonderful. Look at the *piece of chocolate* and, when you are ready, choose one part of it to bring closer to your nose and smell it. If you would like, place it in your mouth and take a small bite. Hold it in your mouth, on your tongue, for a moment. Consider the history of this *piece of chocolate*— what brought it to you at this moment. Consider the workers involved in packing, driving, and placing the *package of chocolate* on the grocery store shelf before you held it in your hand.

When you are ready, chew the *chocolate* until you are ready to swallow, noticing the sensations of your tongue, saliva, and throat. When you swallow, feel the movement of the *piece of chocolate* as it travels from your mouth, down your throat, and into your stomach. Return to your breathing, and notice your breath as it enters and leaves your body.

Now let's talk about your experience. Why do you think I'm asking you to do all these things? Does this exercise make you more aware of your surroundings? Can you imagine why that would be a good thing?

Adaptation for younger children: Younger children very much enjoy this activity, and you can use a raisin instead of chocolate if you are concerned with feeding your child sugary snacks. You can choose to use fewer steps during the activity in order to sustain your child's attention.

---

[8]   Note: You can easily substitute the word "orange" anywhere that the phrase "piece of chocolate" is used in the script.

ACTIVITY

Go Take a Walk

Target age: 11 to 15

Goal: To help your child be mindful of ordinary activities that involve movement, such as walking

Materials needed: None

Script: Let's find a place to take a short walk. It can be anywhere you like—in the park, around the block in our neighborhood, or in the shopping mall or library. As you begin to walk, choose something to focus on, such as a sound. Notice what your senses bring to your attention, and become curious about the sound. Is it loud or soft? Pleasant or annoying? Try to hear the sound and then switch to a different sound, or attend to all of the sounds at once as a larger group of sounds.

   Now, as you continue to walk, notice what you see. Notice the colors, shadows, and movements of the people and things along our walk. Be aware of any thoughts that come to mind as you walk. Are there any patterns or colors that strike you in particular and invite your eyes to linger?

Adaptation for younger children: This activity is suitable for young children, who enjoy exploring their surroundings as much as older children. The first time you do this activity with a younger child, focus her attention on only one of her senses, such as smell. Ask her questions that require her to notice one sense at a time.

There are many casual opportunities for mindfulness. The activity that follows is more a formal, structured mindfulness strategy. Guided meditations may be found online, in books, and on CDs and DVDs.

Ordinary Tasks that Your Child May Engage in Mindfully

Taking a shower or bath	Brushing her teeth
Getting dressed	Washing her hair
Exercising	Walking to the store
Drinking	Playing an instrument

ACTIVITY

Mystic Mountain[9]

Target age: 11 to 15

Goal: To cultivate in your child a sense of competence through mindfulness

Materials needed: A chair or spot on the floor

Script: Let's begin. Find a comfortable position either sitting in a chair or lying on the floor. Let your hands rest comfortably in your lap or by your sides. You may wish to close your eyes or gaze at a spot on the ceiling.

Imagine you are looking at a large mountain—a glorious, beautiful mountain. It may be one that you have seen or visited before, or it might be one that exists only in your imagination. Notice the mountain's overall shape—its sides, peaks, and the slope of the enormous land mass. As the mountain comes into clearer focus, you may notice trees growing on the mountain, animals grazing on it, and perhaps the sun is shining above and snow decorating the higher peaks. See that the mountain is firmly planted in the earth, unmoving and strong.

As you continue to observe it, you realize that you share many qualities of the mountain. You are firmly planted, strong, and beautiful. Imagine that your head is the top of the mountain and you can look around you and survey the area that surrounds you. Your head is supported by the rest of your magnificent body, and your shoulders and arms are the sides of the mountain, descending down to your body's base—to your chair or to your back resting on the floor.

With each breath, you see that the sun and clouds travel across the sky each day, making patterns and shadows that change, just as day turns into night and the stars and moon move across the sky in patterns of their own. The light and shape of the moon changes from a sliver to a half to a full circle, and sometimes the moon is hidden behind the clouds. Each season brings changes to the mountain, too. In summertime there are bright green leaves on the trees, and grass growing on the surfaces of the slopes. In autumn the leaves change color and fall to the ground. During the winter there is snow and ice on the mountaintop and in spaces where the sun's warmth doesn't reach. And in spring, flowers bloom and leaves begin to grow on the trees.

[9] Adapted from Kabat-Zinn, 1990/2013.

The birds' chirping can be heard across the peaks and valleys, and other wildlife is visible as your eyes wander along the mountain's terrain.

Adaptation for younger children: This activity is suitable for young children, but you may wish to simplify the visualization language or shorten the script. There are meditations readily available online and in books, which are designed especially for young children.

As your child begins to develop a greater awareness of herself, she can discover the distinction between her thoughts and feelings. A feeling can elicit a thought. For example, a child may think, "I'm not fast enough to make the cross-country team," and the feeling(s) associated with that thought may be anxiety, frustration, or insecurity. The list below illustrates an assortment of feelings words, divided in categories, that can help spark conversation with your child.

Scared—afraid, anxious, nervous, tense
Angry—annoyed, grumpy, grouchy, seething
Sad—despondent, unhappy, disappointed, incompetent
Happy—jubilant, blissful, excited, optimistic

Some children may benefit from a photo or drawing that clearly illustrates what certain feelings look like. There are wonderful examples of facial expressions that you can find online or in books, and you can easily co-create your own "emotions chart" that provides concrete examples of feelings and what they look like on family members' faces/bodies.

ACTIVITY

Color the Pain Away

Target age: 11 to 15
Goal: To demonstrate to your child the practical usefulness of mindfulness
Materials needed: None

Script: Mindfulness has a lot of very practical uses. The next time you are in pain, try using the strategy I'm going to teach you now. I think you'll be amazed at how well it works.

Do you have a pain in your body right now? No? Okay, let's put one there. Pinch some skin on your arm and then pinch it a little harder until it starts to hurt. I'm sure you know that this pain will be gone before very long, but it will be useful in teaching you this aspect of mindfulness. I want you to concentrate on the spot on your arm that now hurts from your having pinched it. See it as a small circle just underneath your skin. Now imagine that that circle is red—fiery red! Look at it in your mind's eye for a few moments and now notice that the circle is starting to turn yellow. As it goes from red to yellow it starts to mellow a little bit and doesn't hurt as much. Now see it as white. Even less pain. Now blue. Even less pain. And finally, see the circle as green. It is calm and pain free.

You see, pain is something you experience in your mind and body. The nerves in your body send a message to your pain center in your brain, which reacts to protect you when you've hurt yourself. Many times, however, the pain is not useful and you want it to go away. Try picturing it in this series of colors, and I think you'll be amazed at how quickly it calms down and hurts less.

Adjustment for younger children: You may not want your child to induce her own pain in this activity. It will probably be enough to ask her to remember the last time she fell and hurt a part of her body. Make sure that she truly remembers how much it hurt, before you begin the activity above.

The major principles of mindful thinking can be summed up thus:

- You are not your thoughts. In fact, you can learn to be in control of your mind, and thus can choose what you think about (or do not think about!).
- Thoughts are fleeting, like visitors.
- Thoughts result from a combination of factors, including heredity, previous experience(s), and the situation in the moment.

Helping children to be more deeply aware of their own thoughts is vital to success in the 21st century. For example, this self-discovery strategy can foster healthy relationships with others.

ACTIVITY

Your Feelings Thermometer

Target age: 6 to 10

Goal: To help your child is identify how her body is feeling at a given moment

Materials needed: A drawing or picture of a thermometer

Script: Picture a thermometer used to measure the temperature—either outside your house, or inside your own body to see if you have a fever. Some thermometers show numbers that go higher when your body is warmer, and other thermometers show a red line that moves higher up the stick. You can see what it looks like on a thermometer at home, and show your child how the line moves up and down when more or less heat is applied to the tip. Our bodies can tell us how we are feeling in a way that is very similar to a thermometer.

1. Focus on one part of your body—perhaps your neck, your shoulder, your stomach, your head—any part of your body you choose.
2. Bring your attention to feeling the part of your body you want to focus on. What thoughts come up for you? As you breathe, imagine that you are breathing into that part of your body.
3. As you pay attention to your feelings, you may notice that the sensations in your body start to change a little. Your muscles might begin to soften, and you may notice warmth or coldness in that part of your body. Note how high the "bar" is on your feelings thermometer, and notice any changes.

Adaptations for older children: they may simply imagine the image of a thermometer in their minds and speak from that point of reference.

Your child may want to color in a drawing of a thermometer to indicate how she is feeling in general or how a specific body part feels in a given moment. You can use the drawings as conversation starters, which will, over time, provide excellent records for comparison.

Activities that Foster Accurate Decision-Making

If She Could Only Tell Me What's Wrong!
By Lindsey Neves[10]

"Rachel" was attempting vainly to stuff her books, folders, and notebooks into the metal pocket under her desk. Miss Neves had told the students to create a "nice clean space" on their desktops. The instructions that she was about to give would help prepare them for the state test that would occur in four months. The date is a looming presence that all teachers feel—in the lunchroom, in the copy room, in meetings, in articles on the Internet. "Hurry up! Get into these kids' heads! Make it work!"

Rachel kept shoving. Students were starting to look at her. The classroom atmosphere was becoming overwrought. Softly, Miss Neves told her to put the books on the floor. Rachel threw her hands in the air, stomped her feet, and began to sob. "I just can't! I can't make it fit!" Later, Miss Neves would learn that Rachel had been witnessing serious abuse at home, had moved into a small apartment with eight family members, and had been suffering from post-traumatic stress disorder. And here Rachel was being asked to create a "nice, clean space."

As an undergraduate education major, Miss Neves had learned about Bloom's taxonomy, Piaget's stages of development, and Maslow's hierarchy of needs. She knew terms like "scaffolding" and "differentiated instruction." But she could not decide what to do for this girl. And what if Rachel had been given the ability to explain what was going on?

As your child becomes more aware of her feelings, she will be better able to read a given situation, respond to stimuli accurately, and interpret cues from her environment well. The activities that follow will encourage her to pay attention to her feelings and go one step further—to make appropriate decisions. Equipping your child with the vocabulary to articulate her thoughts and feelings, as well as use imagery to understand the ephemeral nature of thoughts and feelings, will strengthen her ability to deal with difficult situations.

[10] Reproduced by kind permission of Lindsey Neves, who is a sixth-grade Language Arts teacher in North Attleboro, MA.

ACTIVITY

Seeing through Feelings Glasses

Target age: 6 to 10

Goal: To help your child recognize her feelings, and to see how they can improve by considering a different perspective

Materials needed: A few pairs of inexpensive low-magnification (1.25) reading glasses (available in most drug stores) or oversized, exaggerated frames made from cardboard and plastic wrap

Script: I have a pair of special glasses. These glasses are so incredible! What makes them so special? Well, when you put on these glasses, they allow you to see the world through happy eyes! Everything is beautiful and people who wear them are always happy.

Are you willing to try the glasses? Great! What do you see? Does the world look like a happy place? Right! People seem happy, and are being kind to each other. Tell me what happens when you speak with someone when you are wearing these glasses.

After a few minutes of thinking and discussion about the happy lenses, switch to a different pair of glasses with different "lenses." You may choose feelings glasses that have one of the following lenses: angry, scared, stubborn, curious, or amazed.

Now would you try wearing this different pair of feelings glasses? They make everyone seem frightened. What happens now?

Do you know people who seem to wear only one type of feelings glasses? Have you ever felt as if your own "feelings glasses" (the imaginary glasses you wear all the time) were foggy—and they sometimes make it difficult for you to focus clearly? Can you see how the feelings you have can make a difference in how you see other people?

Adaptation for older children: Older children will likely better understand the concept of seeing the world through different lenses, and can discuss times they've felt like they were seeing things a certain way because they were influenced by certain feelings. If they could rewind the clock, and revisit a particular situation, how might they have acted if they were seeing the situation through a different lens? Role-playing may help to bring different perspectives into view and prompt discussion.

ACTIVITY

Fleeting Feelings

Target age: 6 to 10
Goal: To help your child recognize that feelings are fleeting and ever-changing
Materials needed: None
Script: Begin by inviting your child or a small group of children to sit with you.
I *used* to [pause], and *now* I [pause]. Did you use to do something that you don't do anymore? Have you ever felt a certain way, and now you feel differently? Can you think of something that has changed over time? See if you can think of examples of "I used to _____, and now I _____."

If there are several children, have each child share her or his responses one at a time. Once all of the responses have been shared, ask what patterns emerge. Point out that sometimes we feel a certain way about something and then we change. For example, we may feel worried about a test. Then our feelings become connected to all tests. But if we can be aware of what we are doing, we don't have to do it anymore. That's one of the best things about mindfulness: we can spot harmful feelings, and then change them.

Adaptation for older children: Older children may write their responses on strips of paper. These strips are then placed on a table, the floor, or a wall and arranged in different order to make patterns visible. Are there common themes from different children? What else do they observe?

ACTIVITY

3l

Where the Thoughts Are

Target age: 6 to 10

Goal: To help your child understand that thoughts may be as familiar as the family members and friends that come in and out of our homes for a visit. And, eventually, they will leave as well!

Materials needed: None

Script: Sometimes our thoughts are welcome, and serve us well. Other times, our thoughts are not welcome—they are like guests in our house who won't leave! We wish they would leave, but they just stay put. Imagine that you become so familiar with your thoughts that you can greet them in your mind, much as you would your aunt or neighbor. You don't need to engage in a conversation with them. Instead, you can simply greet them and then move along.

Share an example with your child to give her an idea of how this might sound.

Let's try an example. Let's say you have an important test tomorrow, and your thought is, "I hope I don't fail!" You might respond to that thought, "Good morning, Aunt Annoying! I've gotta run, see you later!" Another example could be, "What if you don't score a goal in the game tomorrow?" and you respond, "See you later, Mr. Negative! I've got a cookie to eat." The point is, you don't have to let those thoughts upset you. They're only thoughts, after all. You can recognize them, and then send them on their way! I wonder if you could give me an example right now.

Adaptation for older children: Older children can practice responding to real people or to their own thoughts in much the same way, and have the cognitive ability to apply these skills to future situations. You can help your child think about upcoming situations that might cause feelings of stress or anxiety, and then remember a past event in which she succeeded in sticking with her plan. Over time, these experiences will reinforce the confidence that she can persist in spite of unwelcome, fleeting feelings.

A child who is able to practice mindfulness will be better able to remain calm in the face of stressful situations. In the chapter that follows, specific strategies are presented that will promote this element of peace in your child's thinking and being.

Part II

Self-management

4

Resiliency: Calming Fears and Anxiety

If you can keep your head when all about you
Are losing theirs and blaming it on you;
If you can trust yourself when all men doubt you,
But make allowance for their doubting too;
If you can wait and not be tired by waiting,
Or, being lied about, don't deal in lies,
Or, being hated, don't give way to hating,
And yet don't look too good, nor talk too wise;
If you can dream—and not make dreams your master;
If you can think—and not make thoughts your aim;
If you can meet with triumph and disaster
And treat those two imposters just the same;
If you can bear to hear the truth you've spoken
Twisted by knaves to make a trap for fools,
Or watch the things you gave your life to broken,
And stoop and build 'em up with worn out tools;
If you can make one heap of all your winnings
And risk it on one turn of pitch-and-toss,
And lose, and start again at your beginnings

Your Child's Social and Emotional Well-Being: A Complete Guide for Parents and Those Who Help Them, First Edition. John S. Dacey, Lisa B. Fiore, and Steven Brion-Meisels.
© 2016 John Wiley & Sons, Ltd. Published 2016 by John Wiley & Sons, Ltd.
Companion website: www.wiley.com/go/daceywellbeing

And never breathe a word about your loss;
If you can force your heart and nerve and sinew
To serve your turn long after they are gone,
And so hold on when there is nothing in you
Except the Will which says to them: "Hold on";
If you can talk with crowds and keep your virtue,
Or walk with kings—nor lose the common touch;
If neither foes nor loving friends can hurt you;
If all men count with you, but none too much;
If you can fill the unforgiving minute
With sixty seconds' worth of distance run—
Yours is the Earth and everything that's in it,
And—which is more—you'll be a Man, my son!

If, by Rudyard Kipling

Kipling was a 19th-century poet, so we should not be surprised that he uses the chauvinistic "Man." He might have used "Brave Person," but of course that doesn't rhyme. Nevertheless, his words offer a wonderfully cogent definition of cool-headedness under fire.

Another way to describe the topic of *If* is—resiliency in the face of stress. This is one of the most desirable traits in the SEL pantheon, because stressful situations are so common these days. True, other places and periods in history have been equally distressing (Kipling was writing about such a era in India). Nevertheless, as this whole book documents, the tension level is high. And if a child's anxiety level is excessive, *that child cannot think well*.

Every child needs to learn how to bounce back from adversity. The critical first step in achieving resiliency is the ability to calm the mind when tempted to panic. The two most common reactions to stress of all kinds are fear and anxiety.[1] Fear is the feeling you get when you know what it is that is threatening you. Anxiety is the feeling you get when you are threatened, but you are not sure what's really intimidating you. The reactions provoked by either of these two emotions are, however, indistinguishable. Another useful distinction is that the field of psychology recognizes eight categories of anxiety:

- Specific (simple) phobia.
- Social phobia.
- Separation anxiety.

---

[1] Dacey & Fiore, 2000, 2006; Dacey, Fiore, & Brion-Meisels, 2016; Doucette, 2012.

- Agoraphobia.
- Panic disorder.
- Generalized anxiety disorder (GAD).
- Obsessive compulsive disorder (OCD).
- Posttraumatic stress disorder (PTSD).[2]

These anxiety problems are listed in order of severity. Although we do not have the space here to examine each type, you may want to read more about them. That way, you can learn whether your child is a victim of one (or more).

All eight of these anxiety disorders can be found among children and adolescents, and since the advent of terrorist actions, especially against schools, the percentage is growing. In the United States, they are the most common mental illnesses, affecting 18% of the population. They are highly treatable, yet only about one-third of those suffering receive treatment.[3] Sometimes more than one of these disorders may occur at the same time, making it difficult to identify a single disorder. If you suspect one of these syndromes is present in your child, you probably should seek the advice of a licensed psychotherapist or other medical professional.

Although the eight types of anxiety are quite different from each other, they do have one thing in common. They all invoke the "fight-or-flight" response. This lives in an ancient part of the human brain, and three millennia ago it was useful. For example, suppose you are a cave person strolling among a field of boulders, when you glance up at the top of the largest rock and, to your dismay, you spot a crouching saber-toothed tiger. You might say to yourself, "Well, let's see now, what are my options?" This is not a good idea, because while you are thinking you may well become the tiger's lunch. The best options are to grab a stick and attack the tiger, or back away (probably the latter). You should either fight or flee.

In today's world, those two options don't work very well. For example, if you're nervous about giving a speech to a large audience, you might scream at them, "Don't look at me!" or you might run off the stage. Not very good solutions, are they? You would do better to get a grip on yourself and calm down. That's not so easy to do, because the anxiety reaction is so complex. Medicine recognizes 26 different, adrenaline-stoked responses, such as

---

[2] American Psychiatric Association, 2014.
[3] ADAA, 2013.

higher blood pressure and bristling hair on the back of the neck. Nevertheless there are some excellent ways to quiet your nerves. In this chapter we help you teach your child how to handle adversity effectively, and you may want to try a number of them yourself!

ACTIVITY

4A

Biofeedback—Pulse Rate

Biofeedback is a tool that provides some type of data, often electronic, about the human body. The most common indicator is only heart rate or pulse, which rise when a person is under stress. The purpose of biofeedback is to learn how to identify and control thoughts, physical sensations, and behavior. For example, the feeling of a racing heart, even if only from running around, can be scary to a child. This emotion can quickly turn to a belief that something is seriously wrong, even when nothing is. In this thought pattern, the mind–body connection will likely produce poor concentration and an uncomfortable feeling of tension and foreboding.

Target age: 10 to 16

Goal: Develop an unconscious method of calming the anxious mind

Materials needed: Pulse oximeter (on Amazon for $21). Of course you could just take the child's pulse using your fingers and the second hand of your watch. However, the power of this instrument comes from his watching his pulse rate number come down on the oximeter's screen as he uses various calming methods. The oximeter is a simple, portable tool that clips comfortably on a child's fingertip and measures heart rate in real time. This instrument is also available at your local pharmacy or medical supply store for a higher price. Other types of biofeedback machines offer a complex of biological feedback, but they cost much more.

Script: You should approach this exercise as a kind of experiment with your youth. Place the pulse oximeter on his pointer finger and wait a moment or two until the meter registers his pulse rate. Record that number. Track progress over a month's time.

First I am going to put this device onto your finger. Comfortable? I want you to look at your heart rate number on this little monitor. Okay, write it down here on this chart. Now you are going to try to control your feelings simply by changing your thoughts. That will make the number in the window on the monitor go down. Close your eyes, relax and breathe slowly. [Pause.] All set? I'm not going to tell you anything except that your job is to notice your breathing and think about relaxing. That will lower your heart rate. Relax any way you can. Just be aware of your breathing. You can do it! Use the tracking sheet below to record your numbers.

Tracking sheet

Time of day	Situation	Starting pulse rate	End pulse rate	Change	Start hand temperature or GSR level	End hand temperature or GSR level	Change

After a few moments have your child open his eyes and read the pulse rate on the oximeter. Almost certainly, it will be a lower number than before. Tell him to record the new number on the tracking sheet (the last three columns will be used in the next exercise). Compare the two numbers and talk about any differences he feels, physically and emotionally, with a higher versus a lower heart rate. Try this technique again, to see if he can get an even lower number. You can create a tracking record over days or weeks that looks like this.

Practicing during a relaxed time for a period of a few weeks will help your child learn the effects of biofeedback, and understand its value during stressful times. The next step, when he is better at lowering his pulse, is to try this exercise when he is really under serious pressure, such as the day of a big test or some on-stage performance in school. If he can lower his stress level before he leaves for school, he can do it just before the event, and will be more confident and successful.

Adaptation for younger children: Instead of using imagination, show your child a brief video of a calming scene (see our website: www.wiley.com/go/daceywellbeing) and ask him to close his eyes, relax his muscles, and breathe slowly. Otherwise, same as above.

ACTIVITY

 4B

Biofeedback: Hand Temperature (or Galvanic Skin Response—GSR)

The stress response also involves increased sweat gland activity. Hence, frightened people often have cold, clammy hands. Biofeedback training can train the body to achieve a more typical response pattern (warm, dry hands).

Target age: 6 to 10

Goal: Develop an unconscious method of calming an anxious mind

Materials needed: A hand thermometer or GSR sensor does the job. The Stress Thermometer ($22 at Amazon) has the advantage of giving a specific number value for stress levels that can be compared over time to check improvement, but also for degrees of reactions to different stressful events. The GSR sensor is a somewhat more accurate measure of stress, but costs more. For example, the GSR2 ($70 at Amazon) monitors stress levels by translating tiny tension-related changes in skin pores into a rising or falling tone. By resting two fingers on the sensing plates, your child will learn to lower the pitch of the sound the instrument makes, and thus his stress level.

Script: Now we are going to try to help you control your fear level by relaxing your muscles. Let me clip this little cartridge onto two of your fingers [or: Place your fingers into these two grooves.] The best way to relax your muscles is to tighten all of them by making yourself as tense as possible, and then completely letting go. You might feel a little funny when you do this. For example you might scrunch up your eyes, eyebrows, and mouth. It will be easier if you find a private place like a bedroom or bathroom to do it in. [Pause.]

All set? Now squeeze all your muscles, as tight as you can. Hold it while I count to 10. 1, 2, 3, 4, 5, 6, 7, 8, 9, 10. Now let go completely. See how the meter [sound] on the machine shows a lower level of tension [goes down]? Do you feel more relaxed? With practice, you can become more serene even without the biofeedback machine!

Adaptation for older children: As with Activity 4A, do not provide any other information on how to relax. Let your youth use whatever method he likes. You might not even suggest relaxing. Just tell him to try to lower the stress indicator any way he can.

ACTIVITY

Using an Amulet

Target age: 6 to 10
Goal: Calming an anxious mind through empowering objects
Materials needed: An amulet is a symbolic object which can be imbued with calming power, which can then be used to relieve your child's fears. It could be a small stone, a religious medal, or a baked, painted and shellacked heart. Your child could select one of the first two, or help with the last one.
Script: Suppose your child worries about the crash of thunderstorms, or that big dogs might bite him. You and your family have decided that designing a ritual in which you all participate weekly could be a big help to him. You have concluded that an amulet should be the centerpiece of your rite (this ritual worked well for one 5-year-old girl we know).

These are the steps that we suggest you take:

1. Start with a family discussion. Your child needs to see that the family members care about him, and want to take care of him if he agrees to participate in this exercise.

   [Name], your family is gathered here this morning to help you with your fearful feelings. We know you are frightened by snakes and spiders. We love you, and we feel very sad that you're experiencing such fearful feelings. Would you please describe for us what it feels like?

   For example, he might say he is afraid a snake or a spider is going to attack him and suck out all his blood. Who wouldn't be scared if they thought that might happen?

2.   Ask family members to help your child pick or design the amulet, as well as to plan the ritual within which it will be strengthened. One approach would be to take him to a hobby store where they sell a variety of beads with holes in them. Tell him to pick out enough beads to make a 6-inch bracelet. The bracelet then becomes his amulet. He might wear it all of the time (inside or outside his sleeve, as he wishes), or only when he feels afraid. During the family ritual, the bracelet should receive the good wishes, hopes, and/or prayers of all the family members.

3.   The empowering of the amulet should take place at the end of each week until the ritual sessions have done their job: the amulet has eliminated the overwhelming fear (there still may be some nervous feelings when a spider appears, but they are manageable). The family might hold a discussion with child about how his week has gone. Then say,

> Have you had fearful feelings this week [such as when we spotted a snake when we went hiking last Saturday]? What did you do when you were scared? Did your bracelet help? Did you imagine all of us being with you, protecting you from harm?

Family members should be sympathetic with his feelings without agreeing that such a fear is inevitable. If he wishes, they should offer him suggestions about how he might be more successful in dealing with his anxiety in the week to come.

4.   Finally, at each session, there is the re-empowering of the amulet. All family members put their hands on it simultaneously, and while touching it, each person speaks lovingly of him and the wish/hope/prayer that he will be freed from these fearful feelings.

Adaptation for older children: An older child might be more comfortable with a ritual that he creates himself in the privacy of his own room. He may be embarrassed by his need for the amulet. It should still be empowered by the family, but it might be kept in a small, special box on his bedside table and worn only when he goes in the woods or a field.

ACTIVITY

Visualization

Target Age: 11 to 15
Goal: To release tension through visualizations
Materials needed: None
Script: The ability to visualize, which may include mental notions of taste and touch as well as sight, is truly vital to anxiety control. The ability to imagine physical conditions and desired outcomes plays a role in a number of the techniques we are recommending in this book.

Our research has found that inner-city children are less skilled in this area than suburban youngsters.[4] In fact, inner-city children are less likely to have been asked to imagine things in general—this is not a priority when there are more urgent needs that must be met. Relaxation in general and control of anxiety in particular demand good visualizing skills, and the only way to get them is through practice.

Here are some images we have used in our research on the visualization abilities of students. You may want to try these images yourself or with your child:

- "Can you see your own name clearly in your mind?"
- "Can you spell it backwards?"
- "Can you spell 'bus stop' backwards with your eyes closed?"
- "Can you picture what an elephant looks like?"
- "What kind of ears does it have?"
- "How many notches does it have on its trunk?"

Adaptation for younger children: You may choose to use the list reactions from children's books in a similar manner.

---

[4] Dacey, Amara, & Seavey, 1993.

ACTIVITY

"Ouch!"

Target age: 11 to 15
Goal: To use sensory experience to stifle negative thoughts
Materials needed: Strong rubber band, placed around one wrist
Script: Ask your child to wear a rubber band around his wrist and snap it gently against the inside skin as soon as he imagines something frightening is happening to him. Most children find that this soon eliminates their obsessive thinking, because their minds quickly associate the anxious thoughts with the uncomfortable sting, and avoid it. As with other methods used to vent emotions, you need to be careful that this activity does not itself provoke anxiety.

Adaptation for younger children: A less painful alternative might be some boring task such as turning the hands of a watch 12 hours forward or reciting a long, dull poem. If the child forces himself to perform a boring activity each time the catastrophic thought occurs, a negative association will gradually eliminate it.

ACTIVITY

Scale Your Fears

Target age: 11 to 15
Goal: To interrupt your child's anxious obsessions and reduce their severity. Creating a fear scale allows you and your child to chart fearful episodes. Over time, this tends to help him recover.
Materials needed: Index cards, pen or pencil
Script: Write down two of your fearful experiences, the worst ones you've had. Describe them on two 3″ × 5″ cards. Assign a score of 10 to incidents like that. Now try to recall two situations when you were completely relaxed.

Explain what it felt like on two of the cards. Those are labeled 1. Finally, try to think of two times when you felt halfway between these two extremes. Those are level 5 anxieties. Write them on two other cards. Now you have examples you can compare to what happens the next time you feel anxious.

Now write the following headings written atop columns across the 5" side:

Data recording sheet

Date	Anxiety	Feelings	Thoughts

Any time your child experiences anxiety above level 3, he should find a private place and fill out a line on the card as soon as possible. Performing the self-analysis this task requires will help to calm him. Even more important, it will help him establish a documented pattern that will be invaluable in creating imaginative plans for handling the situation in the future (more on this in Chapter 11).

Adaptation for young children: If your child is just beginning to write, he can dictate his feelings for you to write on the cards. Ask him to pick an appealing scene from one of his favorite books. Then have him pick a scene that he finds frightening. Continue picking scenes of each kind until he has an array of scenes that he can rank from high to low. You can then discuss with him why he made those ratings, a wonderful source of insights for you!

ACTIVITY

The Yogic Sponge

Target age: 6 to 15
Goal: To reach a deep state of relaxation and emotional serenity
Materials needed: Exercise mat, thick blanket, or rug

Script: First suggest to your child that he begin by lying down on a firm but cushioned surface, such as a rug. Read this script in a soft, soothing voice. It is written for older children and teens, so the script will need to be simplified for younger children. You may want to record your reading so that your child can play the tape whenever he wishes.

Lie down on a soft place. Put your hands beside you with your palms down, then let them turn up by themselves naturally. Let your feet spread apart a little bit. Get stretched out and try to get yourself in a nice relaxed position. The idea is to go on a mental trip. Instead of going on a trip away from home, you're going into the deepest part of yourself, your own personal home. This is a time specifically just for you, nobody else. You're going to be thinking only about getting yourself into position, so that you can do some really good relaxing. [Pause.]

Concentrate on your feet, especially your toes. Wiggle them around a little bit. Tense your feet up a little bit if you want to, pull them toward you and then just let them go. Let them just relax completely. That's really good. [Pause.]

Now let this feeling of relaxation spread up into your ankles, shinbones, up to your knees. You may want to straighten your legs out and bend them just a little bit. Make sure the tightness is out of your knees, then let this mellow feeling move up your thighs. Your muscles are letting go and now your legs are starting to become very, very heavy. They are pressing down against the rug and maybe almost through the rug. It feels wonderful to just lie there and sink deeper into this state of serenity. [Pause.]

This feeling now is beginning to spread up into your hips and your lower abdomen, up into your stomach. It is beginning now to filter into your chest. Notice that as you start to relax, breathing now becomes slower. In fact, you can take a deep breath, hold it for a while and let it go. Try it now—I'll count so that you can tell how long to do each of these three tasks.

First let all your breath out—*all* your breath. Now you're going to inhale, one, two, three, four, five, six, seven, eight, let it out, two, three, four, five, six, seven, eight, hold it two, three, four, five, six, seven, eight. As you practice this, you're going to become just like a sponge, just lying there soaking things up. You want to get your breathing to start to become slower and slower and deeper and deeper. Not just in your chest, but down in your belly. [Pause.]

Now let the feeling spread into your shoulders. Scrunch your shoulders up a little bit, wiggle them around, and make sure that they really let go.

Let them "fall" into the floor, so that your entire body now feels very, very heavy. [Pause]

This feeling of heaviness is starting to move through your shoulders into your upper arms, down through your elbows and now it's flowing down into your forearms. Your arms are becoming very heavy. [Pause.]

This feeling is now going into your palms, the backs of your hands, slowly going out through your fingers and your thumbs, a feeling of heaviness and deep relaxation. [Pause] Now return back up through your shoulders and into your neck. [Pause.]

Let this feeling come up through your chin, up through the back of your head and into your face. Your mouth is probably a little bit open, because you're doing nice deep breathing in through your nose and out through your mouth, feeling it up through your nose and cheekbones, even your ears. Concentrate on total, total relaxation. [Pause]

Next check your eyes and make sure that they're just barely closed. Let this feeling of relaxation go up now through your forehead. It's a very lovely heavy feeling. The feeling is now up through your scalp and you're extremely relaxed. [Pause.]

Your whole body feels like a heavy rock. It's very pleasant. You have no responsibilities except to make yourself relax. Now I would like you to concentrate on that part of your face that is directly between your eyes and the top of your nose. Imagine that a magical golden fluid is starting to pour into your head through this special opening in the center of your forehead, down right between your eyes. You feel a golden yellow liquid, like honey, a warm relaxing fluid, just tremendously relaxing as it moves into your head now and fills your head and down through your neck. [Pause.]

You feel it flowing down inside, down through your shoulders and your arms, through your hands. It gives you total peace. Now it's starting to flow to fill your entire upper body, starting to flow into your legs. Slowly but surely you feel this warm, relaxing sensation surge down through you, down through your knees, down through your shins and your calves, total relaxation and a sense of safety and peace. Total peace floods through you and now down through your ankles into your feet, all the way through your feet down to your toes. And now your entire body is filled with this serene, warm, golden fluid. [Pause, then speak in a slightly softer voice.]

Instead of feeling heavy, now, you notice that you've developed a lightness, as though you're floating. You're completely relaxed. You're thinking of nothing but the warm, very comfortable feeling that you're getting from this.

And you're sinking down into it. You're letting yourself just be filled with this. You hear my voice very well, but it seems like it's from far away. And you find yourself drifting farther and farther away. You're thinking of nothing, nothing at all, but the peace that's there. You may want to picture a scene, like looking at the ocean or some other beautiful place. You do not feel sleepy, you do not feel tired at all, you feel just very, very comfortable, quite safe, at peace. [Pause.]

You're filled with peacefulness, you're filled with the wonderful sense of freedom. Nothing's bothering you at all. You're at peace. You are now down in a very special, safe place, deep inside yourself, completely relaxed and completely safe. [Pause.]

All right, now start to think about coming back up to the surface again. You feel yourself sort of floating back up. You have become so light and free that you're actually floating. As you start to re-enter the "outside world," you may want to just wiggle a finger. Do it slowly, at your own pace. Slowly come back. Move your feet around a little bit if you want to. As you feel ready to do it, open your eyes. Eventually you may want to get up on one elbow. [Pause.]

Gradually get yourself up to a sitting position. And get ready, because I'm going to turn the light back on. Now think back. Do you feel calmer? Happier? More mentally alert? Would you like to do this again sometime?

ACTIVITY

Bonus for Parents

During which part of the day do most of us experience anxiety? That's right, for most of us, it's the morning. In part, that's because we spend our sleeping hours replenishing our supply of adrenaline, which was depleted by the stressors of the previous day. When we have burned off a majority of our supply, by afternoon, we may experience a mild depression.

Adrenaline plays a large role in our emotional mood states, but so does food. You can't do much about your hormonal condition without serious medications, but you can decide what you eat and when. It's not always easy, but it's so worth the effort.

Nutritional science tells us that sugars and most carbohydrates turn immediately into energy by causing a spike in our blood sugar (through the release of adrenaline). This is hard on our pancreas, which must produce enough insulin to balance the spike. Known as "homeostasis," the body works hard to return to a more normal state. When we eat a glazed donut and coffee with cream and sugar for breakfast, KAPOW! We first feel a pleasant jolt, but then, as our sugar level quickly rises, we experience tension and a vague sense that all is not well. When we feel that way, it is easy to find an object for our worry. Job security, a troublesome student, a personal relationship—any normal concern can be exacerbated by stress. And stress interferes with our ability to deal effectively with the disruption.

Then comes lunch, usually consisting of more proteins and fats, with much less sugar content. Our blood sugar level flattens, and begins to decline. Not surprisingly, mild depression sometimes ensues. A common reaction by mid-afternoon is "This job is frustrating! What am I doing here?"

The solution? At all three meals (never skip any!), you should try to eat something from each of these food groups: proteins; fats; carbohydrates (includes fruit and sugars); and vegetables. It's important to eat enough proteins, especially for breakfast, to balance sugar spikes. This might mean a strip or two of bacon, but low-fat meats like chicken and turkey, or even a high-protein bar are usually better alternatives.

You will also need to have two snacks per day, each composed of foods from two of the four groups. Finally, check with a certified nutritionist, at least for one session. This person will analyze your eating habits, explain in more detail how it all works, and advise you on what you need to do. Do not make the mistake of thinking you already know about the science of eating. It has advanced in recent years, and you will probably learn a lot. You're worth it!

Of course, this goes for children, too. A child without sugar spikes is a calm child. A calm child is one who can think clearly. A clear-thinking child can draw on all of his remembered experiences and also his unconscious resources to solve his problems. This in turn allows him to make judgments independent from his anxieties, a major goal of SEL.

5

Independent Thinking

So here's why I changed my mind. It wasn't so I wouldn't have to hear Mom give me a whole lecture. And it wasn't to protect this August kid from Julian, who I knew would be a jerk about the whole thing. It was because when I heard Jamie talking about how he had run away from August going "Ahhh," I suddenly felt really bad. The thing is, there are always going to be kids like Julian who are jerks. But if a little kid like Jamie, who's usually a nice enough kid, can be that mean, then a kid like August doesn't stand a chance...[1]

On the most basic level, being able to think independently means not being overly influenced by others' opinions. For children, this can mean standing up for a classmate who's being teased or choosing pink even though some say it's a "baby" color. Adults have the benefit of life experiences from which we realize that the world doesn't fall in on us when we make mistakes, and we usually are more comfortable taking moderate risks. It is through taking moderate risks that we all learn to analyze situations, calculate an appropriate response, and follow our instincts. With practice, children can be taught to

---

[1] Palacio, 2012.

Your Child's Social and Emotional Well-Being: A Complete Guide for Parents and Those Who Help Them, First Edition. John S. Dacey, Lisa B. Fiore, and Steven Brion-Meisels.
© 2016 John Wiley & Sons, Ltd. Published 2016 by John Wiley & Sons, Ltd.
Companion website: www.wiley.com/go/daceywellbeing

trust their own judgment—to think independently and lead as well as follow. Children can be protagonists as they direct their own life stories.

The concept of leadership will be discussed extensively in Chapter 10. In this chapter it is important to recognize some of the influences on your child's judgments. For example, there are various social and cognitive factors that play into children's inclinations. In the social realm, there is a fundamental sense of belonging that has been argued by theorists[2] as vital to healthy and successful development. Belongingness is reflected in a child's general trust in others, in her comfort in being similar to as well as different from peers, and in a perceived hierarchy in her relationships As she develops, her social group exerts more influence than her parents.

Some researchers suggest that the ability to think is not the same as intelligence. For example, psychologist Edward deBono asserts that "[H]ighly intelligent people are not always good thinkers ... Intelligence is a potential. Thinking is the skill with which we use that potential."[3] The majority of children's formal instruction and social interaction occur in the context of school. Thoughtful critics of the current world educational climate identify independent thinking as a quality of utmost importance if we want to nurture a society that is creative, constructive, and collaborative:

> the purpose of education is to help create people who can think for themselves. Which means we don't care how they look. How they behave. How they learn. How they dream. How they think. We just want to ensure that they do think. Deeply. And for themselves.[4]

Your child's development is also impacted by an environment that teaches "limited thinking skills involved in information sorting and analysis."[5] This tends to be the focus of most school curricula, as opposed to encouraging children to "re-read and re-write the world."[6] Supporting your child's social and emotional development means encouraging her to celebrate her ideas, even if those ideas are different from those of others (especially yours!). SEL invites everyone to the dance.

---

[2] e.g., Maslow, 1954
[3] deBono, 1993.
[4] Gilbert, 2014.
[5] deBono, 1993.
[6] Freire, 2000.

Activities that Foster Exploration

As corporate guru Edward deBono says,

> I have often defined thinking as: "the operating skills with which intelligence acts upon experience." ... one thinker sees the situation and instantly judges it. Another thinker sees the situation, then proceeds to explore the situation and only then proceeds to judge it. The highly intelligent person may carry out the "seeing" and "judging" very well indeed, but if the "exploring" is absent that is bad thinking.[7]

The following activities encourage your child to develop comfort with exploring new situations through a different lens, and to practice feeling comfortable with the uncertainty that often precedes creative problem-solving (see Chapter 11).

ACTIVITY

5A

More than a Guess!

Target age: 11 to 15

Goal: To encourage your child to create tentative explanations about what she observes

Materials needed: Writing materials (paper and pen/pencil, your own electronic device); ice cube and plate or dish

Script: What can you tell me about ice? What do you know about an ice cube? [Your child will respond with some ideas.] What do you think will happen if we leave the ice cube on the table like this? [Your child will respond.]

Explain to your child the difference between a prediction, an educated guess, and a hypothesis. A hypothesis is an explanation about something you're noticing, or a problem that you can investigate further. For example, you might notice that an ice cube will melt if left

---

[7] deBono, 1993.

on a table for a long time. Is this always true? How can you change the hypothesis to make it even more specific so that you can test your ideas, and investigate further? Your child may respond with ideas such as *An ice cube will melt quicker if left on a table in a warm room than in a cold room*, or *An ice cube made from tap water will melt quicker than an ice cube made from orange juice*. These ideas can be tested, observed, and reflected upon. See how many variations your child can come up with, and how far you might stretch her thinking about what seems such a simple phenomenon.

Adaptation for younger children: You can write down your child's words and ideas, and help scaffold her questioning by making connections between ideas if she doesn't notice them herself. She might draw pictures to document her ideas and track the changes in the ice cube(s).

ACTIVITY

Questions, Questions, and More Questions

Target age: 11 to 15

Goal: To teach your child to search for deeper explanations in seemingly simple understandings. The aim is to do this in a way that arouses your child's thinking, rather than stifles it, and bolsters her self-esteem, rather than undermines it

Materials needed: No materials necessary, although paper/pencil or a dry erase board can help record the flow of ideas

Script: You may have heard the name Socrates before. He lived over 2,500 years ago in Greece, and when people speak about him today, it's often because of the way he taught people to think, and to ask themselves questions about what they think. He developed a method for this kind of thinking, which is now called the Socratic method, or dialogue. When two people speak together, that's a dialogue, and that's exactly what Socrates was encouraging people to do—to question each other to get to the heart of their true beliefs and understandings.

You can then choose one of the following prompts to begin a Socratic dialogue with your child, or come up with one of your own:

What does it mean to be good?
What is our responsibility to the Earth?
What makes someone a hero?
How does someone prove she's smart?

The idea here is to begin with a question that seems rather simple and straightforward, and through the process of questioning and questioning again, you and your child will chisel away at your own thoughts until there is no longer any room for contradiction or questioning. Sometimes this takes a long time, and sometimes it moves more quickly. Here is an example of how it might flow:

ADULT: What makes someone a hero?

CHILD: When you risk your own safety for someone else, you're a hero.

ADULT: What if you don't need to risk your own safety, but are perfectly safe? Are you no longer a hero, even if you perform the same act?

CHILD: If you don't risk anything, then anyone could do it. It's only when someone could get hurt or embarrassed that it makes it different.

ADULT: So if there is danger involved, then it's heroic. Are there ordinary acts of heroism that don't involve danger?

CHILD: I guess giving someone food is ordinary, and not really dangerous, and that can be heroic if the person receiving the food is really hungry.

ADULT: Does it matter whether a person does something in public, or can someone be a hero privately or anonymously?

CHILD: Most of the time heroes, like Superman or Spiderman, are doing things in public, and even get in the newspaper—and I know they're not real. I think people can do things behind the scenes that make a difference in people's lives, and if those actions make a big difference, then that's heroic.

ADULT: Does someone need to do something big to be a hero, or can it be something small?

This type of exchange continues until everyone feels content that it's a natural resting point, or if they are ready to move on to something else. The goal is to stimulate your child's thinking and to examine ideas from different angles than one that's most obvious or agreed upon.

ACTIVITY

Ready, Set, Go (and Stay)!

Target age: 11 to 15

Goal: To encourage your child to take an active interest in her world, and to share your own interest in world events and issues

Materials needed: Newspapers and/or magazines such as *Time, National Geographic, Smithsonian,* or other print materials that feature current events from a global perspective; scissors; tape or glue; pencil/pen; paper

Script: Sit with your child and see what catches your eye among the print materials you have with you. Encourage your child to explore the materials, too. Each of you can select, circle, or cut out images or stories that are interesting to you. Negative news events are just as good as positive ones Once you have a few items of interest, say to your child:

Now I'd like you to take a moment to tape or glue your choices to this paper, and I'll do the same. Let's each think about why we picked the ones we picked. We can each write down some words or ideas about what we find really interesting or compelling about each of our choices and then we'll share them with each other.

When you've each had a chance to share what struck you as interesting and exciting, you can follow this up with a question:

Think of some challenges in the world. What are you most passionate about? What can you do about it?

This opens up a channel for discussion with your child about where her interests lie, and new ideas that might come bubbling up. The more conversation you have together, the better able you are to support her interests and strengths, and look for connections between your own interests as well.

Adaptation for younger children: For younger children:

What makes you most happy? Sad? Excited? Curious?

As your child becomes more comfortable taking moderate risks and trusting her own ideas, she will be better able to evaluate the world around her with integrity. This is due to her ability to let go of her ego and the need to be correct, and to appreciate the value of being creative and constructive. In order for a child to develop the self-confidence and self-esteem needed for thinking independently, she must be able to generate a number of ideas from which to choose and explore.

American journalist and satirist Ambrose Bierce defined the brain as "an apparatus with which we think what we think."[8] Most people would agree that if a child's brain works well, then she has a better chance of making sound decisions. It follows that if a child's brain is not working well, then she might make less ideal, and sometimes harmful, decisions. Many factors contribute to children's thinking, and it has been suggested that what we think of as free will is largely an illusion: much of the time, we are simply operating on automatic pilot, and the way we think and act—and how well we think and act on the spur of the moment—is a lot more susceptible to outside influences than we realize."[9]

Some of these outside influences have a strong impact on our judgments, whether it is how much we like the color of someone's tie, or what box we check off on a standardized text next to a prompt for "race/ethnicity." Researchers have noted this "mental contamination"[10] as often harmless (i.e., marketing campaigns), but often damaging (i.e., lower self-esteem). A goal for promoting healthy SEL is to encourage a child to think independently *and* appreciate the multiple perspectives that help inform her thinking.

Activities that Foster Multiple Perspectives

The following activities encourage your child to think about ideas that no one else is thinking. If we want children to think like everyone else, then there is no need to think "outside the box." If we want children to experiment with new ideas, then they need to develop strategies that challenge and extend what is predictable.

---

[8]   Bierce, 2014.
[9]   Gladwell, 2005.
[10] Gladwell, 2005; Marcus, 2008; and Greenfield, 2011.

ACTIVITY

Your Twisted Tongue

Target age: 11 to 15

Goal: To encourage your child to stretch her thinking beyond the predictable, and to tap into creative uses for words and ideas

Materials needed: None

Script: This activity can be done with a small group of children or with an individual child. If you are able to gather a small group of children, the activity will turn into a hilarious exercise, and one that is fun to record with audio or video. With them, you can set up the activity by writing or typing and printing out a few tongue-twisters. Here are some examples:

Three free throws.
A proper copper coffeepot.
She sells seashells by the seashore.
Purple paper people.

These can be taped to the wall in different parts of the room. Tell the group:

One at a time, you will go over to the wall and read one of the tongue-twisters to yourself. Then, you'll come back to the group and tell it to us. Each person in the group will then write down what she heard, and then we'll share with each other.

This is similar to the "telephone" party game, where someone whispers a message to a neighbor sitting in a circle, and this is repeated until it gets back to the original sender.

  If you are working with one child, then you can provide her with a tongue-twister that's written on a piece of paper with some words missing. Her job is to fill in the blanks with words that make sense—serious or silly. For example,

Betty bought some _____ for her batter. Betty's _____ made her batter _____

or

She sells sea_____ by the sea_____

may be used as prompts for your child.

Adjustment for younger children: Children of all ages are able to enjoy this, even if they don't know the "correct" or expected words that fit into the tongue-twister. You can assist with the reading of the tongue-twister and write their words to fill in the blanks accordingly, if needed. Young children are more than up to the challenge!

As children develop, they encounter traditions and stories that provide answers to questions in many areas. These explanations may be shared formally, as in a school setting, or informally, from sibling to sibling or friend to friend. Turning these accepted "truths" upside-down allows your child to consider alternatives. This type of thinking is helpful as children refine their own ability to think independently and not accept something as truth without examining it from many angles. As with the Socratic dialogue activity (5B), younger and older children can participate in this activity with simple modifications to the questions and topics, based on their own interests and knowledge.

ACTIVITY

What If the Opposite Were True?

Target age: 6 to 10
Goal: To encourage your child to consider alternatives to generally accepted stories or values
Materials needed: None are required, but favorite children's books can provide concrete images and language to draw upon, as needed
Script: Here are some suggested conversation starters to choose from:

- *Familiar endings to well-known stories*
  What if Cinderella didn't marry the prince?
  What if Superman was exposed as Clark Kent?
  What if Harry Potter didn't defeat Voldemort?

What if the Hulk emerged when Bruce Banner got extremely happy instead of angry, and his strength increased with the level of happiness?

- *Familiar phenomena*
  What if rain fell up, not down?
  What if elephants were tiny and mice were huge?
  What if we ate cake and ice cream for dinner and carrots and broccoli for dessert?

There are times when, as a result of weighing multiple perspectives and considering paths of action, a child knows she must make a decision that might not be pleasant, but will have a better long-term outcome. Similarly, there are times when a child does not have time to weigh her options, but must instead act quickly and trust her instincts. When your child finds herself in this zone, she needs to believe strongly in the power of her own convictions.

Activities that Foster Conviction in One's Instincts

It is helpful for parents to encourage their child's developing understandings about the world, and to validate her instincts, gently correcting misperceptions and misinformation while supporting her inquisitive spirit. Fictional third-grader Justin Case shares his thoughts about how children are expected to behave and think a certain way, even when it doesn't make sense. His words capture typical childhood assumptions, and resonate with grown-ups who also wonder about the sense behind some dominant opinions:

Hurdles are this thing that's like running but watch out because whoops, in your way there are—I am not even joking—metal fence parts. Which obviously you should just go around. But no. That is not true in camp. You have to somehow just jump right on over the fences. Like you are a cow and the fence is the moon.

As I was running toward the first hurdle, I was thinking about that nursery rhyme and why would people teach that to a kid? A cow can't jump over the moon. A cow can't jump over anything. There is so much kids need to learn in life, and they are new on the planet, so it is kind of mean to waste their time teaching them a cow jumps over the moon.[11]

The following activities promote examination and analysis, and the ability of a child to question "what is" as she considers "what could be."

ACTIVITY

Justice vs. Just Is

Target age: 11 to 15

Goal: To invite your child to offer her opinion on an event that had a particular outcome

Materials needed: Newspaper, magazine, or nonfiction book that illustrates a recent or historical event

Script: Find an example from your materials that is compelling to your child. It could be something as simple as the headline, "School Lunch Prices Increase by $0.50," or the more complex "Drone Testing Allowed in City Neighborhood. Who gets to decide?"

As your child comes up with answers, you may provide insights based on your own knowledge of the situation and your own life experiences. Other prompts may include:

Do you agree with the decision to _____?
Who can you speak with when you don't agree with a decision?
What would happen if people didn't follow this decision?

Adaptation for younger children: You might assume that younger children won't be able to engage in this activity, but you might be surprised at how readily they are able to offer their opinions and justify them with concrete reasoning! If your child feels particularly interested in a topic that comes up in your conversations, encourage her—with help from you as necessary—to write a letter to the newspaper or author of a book to share her ideas about a specific decision or outcome.

---

[11]   Vail, 2012.

ACTIVITY

 5G

Honor Your Instincts

Target age: 11 to 15
Goal: To help your child recognize and honor her instincts, and to validate her knowledge of the world
Materials needed: None, although paper and pen/pencil are helpful to record ideas
Script: Begin by inviting your child or a small group of children to sit with you.

Trusting our instincts can actually save lives when we're in difficult situations, and the media is full of stories that cause us to think "If only they'd followed their instincts!" But trusting one's gut isn't only something for problems or tragedies. There are many examples of famous, successful people—like the late Steve Jobs—who attribute their successes to following their instincts.

Teaching your child to notice and honor her instincts will help her practice this skill so that she may draw upon her own inner wisdom in ordinary and unusual circumstances.

Can you think of a time when you knew something was the right thing to do, and you followed your instinct?

If she has a hard time thinking of an example, you can change the question to,

Can you think of a time when you had a feeling something wasn't right, or you had doubts, and you listened to your inner thinking? Or maybe you decided not to follow your instinct—what happened then?"

Adaptation for younger children: Questions can be adjusted for younger children:

What happens when you have a feeling about something? Do you listen to your ideas? Do you sometimes question whether you are right or wrong?

As you discuss your child's memories and ideas about trusting her gut, you can discuss with her some strategies to help validate her instincts. These include:

- *Quiet your mind.* It's easier to pay attention to your instincts when you are able to find some quiet time to notice them. Try to find a few minutes each day to be someplace quiet, to notice your breathing (inhaling and exhaling), and to turn off electronic devices. Focus your thinking on your breath, and you will naturally calm your mind and notice your thoughts and ideas.
- *Notice your body and what it's telling you.* Sometimes your body is able to tell you something before you even have any thoughts about it! Your body has a wonderful way of telling you when you feel nervous, sad, angry, and other feelings. Notice when you have a headache or stomach ache, or if you have trouble sleeping or eating. You can also focus on how your body responds to certain people you may encounter. Does seeing someone in particular cause you to feel something in your stomach, chest, or head? Noticing and listening to these sensations lets us realize much we know about ourselves and the world, even if we don't think about it at first.
- *Think about your dreams.* Sometimes we remember our dreams, and sometimes it seems like we don't dream at all. When we do wake up and remember a dream, it may sometimes seem connected to real events and thoughts we have, and other times it may seem like nonsense! However, our dreams can give us insight into our thoughts and feelings when we're not aware of them. If there is something on your mind, or that you're worrying about, see if you can make any connections to your dreams and those thoughts or feelings. It can be helpful to keep a notebook or voice recorder near your bed so that you can keep track of your dreams. You can also share dreams with your family during mealtimes. Sometimes sharing with others helps, because other people can see connections that you might miss!

Adaptation for younger children: Younger children can also participate in such discussions. Their ideas and ability to articulate their feelings might be different, and yet the benefit of sharing and connecting with others who share similar experiences makes this a useful exercise.

As we encourage children to think independently, we are also teaching them to question authorities. "[T]he first step to being creative is not an act of creation, or even destruction, as Picasso would have it, but one of refusal."[12] Think of the scene in the film *Dead Poets Society*, when Robin Williams's character, Mr. Keating, is guiding the students through an exercise about conformity. He points out that when he asked a small group of boys to walk, it took only a few seconds for them all to walk in a synchronized manner, to conform to a group walk while the rest of the class clapped in time with their steps. He acknowledges the challenge of maintaining one's own beliefs, saying, "We all have a great need for acceptance, but you must trust that your beliefs are unique, your own, even though the herd may go, 'That's baaaad.'" He then quotes from Robert Frost's poem "The Road Not Taken,"[13] and encourages them to try to find their own unique walk. One student stands off to the side, and when Mr. Keating invites him to join in, he responds that he is "Exercising the right not to walk." Mr. Keating replies, "Thank you, Mr. Dalton. You just illustrated the point."

ACTIVITY

The "Right" of Refusal

Target age: 6 to 15
Goal: To encourage your child to think of alternative behavior when she chooses not to pursue what is suggested
Materials needed: A board game such as Monopoly, Life, Candyland, or Pay Day—a game that can provide your child with useful visuals of a path with many steps

No doubt you have been faced with a situation where you thought to yourself how much more productive it would be if someone offered a suggestion for a solution instead of simply refusing to cooperate. If you have a board game available, you can show your child how making one

12   Gilbert, 2014.
13   Frost, 1916.

decision takes her down one path, and another decision, while somewhat riskier, may actually move her closer to her goal. You may wish to play the board game with your child, pausing to share examples with her of your own thinking and strategizing. Point out instances where you:

- Choose to obstruct her progress in order to advance
- Choose to take a modest risk to progress
- Weigh a decision between two equally appealing/unappealing decisions

Encourage your child to ask questions if she doesn't understand your choices, and to argue for a different decision. The "right" of refusal is an opportunity to prove oneself correct when others would choose differently. Being able to offer explanations for different solutions promotes respect for others' opinions and valuing of disparate ideas.

> The only way that human beings could ever have survived as a species for as long as we have is that we've developed … [a] decision-making apparatus that's capable of making very quick judgments based on very little information.[14]

There are moments in our lives when we choose to (or are forced to) make decisions that are not popular, or that seem wild and unconventional. The ability to think independently does not mean thinking frivolously or without regard for others' feelings and expertise. Thinking independently celebrates the autonomy of mind and spirit that act together and make us capable of rich, colorful human experiences. Author Ian Gilbert encourages us to "Do things no one does or do things everyone does in a way no one does."[15] The world will be all the more exciting if we follow those instructions.

In the chapter that follows, we present information to help your child develop strategies of self-regulation. These skills will help your child achieve a positive balance that further supports her successful, healthy development.

---

[14] Gladwell, 2005.
[15] Gilbert, 2014.

6

Self-regulating

Old Abe, the Rock

Abraham Lincoln, the sixteenth and probably the best president in U.S. history, is an excellent model of self-regulation. *He needed it!* Here's why:

- All his life, he suffered from bouts of depression. It is alleged that when his girlfriend Ann Rutledge died when he was 22, he went to bed in the home of a friend for six months. As a young man, he couldn't control his grief.
- A self-described "homely fellow"—6′ 4″ tall when the average man was 5′ 9″, he was a slender, ungainly man who lacked the social graces American politicians needed. His wife, Mary Todd, the daughter of a leading southern family, was asked how she met him. "He came up to me at a ball," she recalled, "and said he wanted to dance with me in the worst way. Then he did!"
- Two of his sons died in childhood, and his wife became mentally ill. He handled these traumas with genuine self-deprecation.
- With little political and no military experience, he was elected to lead the United States through the most devastating four years in its history. He suffered greatly at the news of the many lost battles

Your Child's Social and Emotional Well-Being: A Complete Guide for Parents and Those Who Help Them, First Edition. John S. Dacey, Lisa B. Fiore, and Steven Brion-Meisels.
© 2016 John Wiley & Sons, Ltd. Published 2016 by John Wiley & Sons, Ltd.
Companion website: www.wiley.com/go/daceywellbeing

and the thousands of soldiers killed, and could hardly bear signing the orders putting traitors to death.

Asked how he felt about being president, he answered, "I feel like the feller who was tarred and feathered and asked how he liked it. The man replied, 'If it weren't for the honor of the thing, I'd sooner forgo it!'"
Throughout the four horrible years of the Civil War, his sense of humor made people love him. He virtually never lost control of his emotions during these trying times. Wouldn't you like your children to be like him? How did he do it?

What Self–regulation Means

Most artists are slovenly, and most scientists look like they have springs coming out of their heads. Both are wildly eccentric, and neither can focus on anything but themselves. They are so intent on their big ideas, the rest of their lives are a mess!

Are these three statements true? As with all stereotypes, some exemplary people are like this. Not many, though. Our research[1] and that of others[2] has found that most highly talented people are, in their personal habits, pretty much like the rest of us. This is because gifted individuals tend to have a higher than usual ability to control their emotions and behavior.[3] And that is because, no matter how innovative their creations, people won't want to hear from the innovator if he is emotionally or socially inappropriate. Without SEL, even the most pioneering person will make little progress with his ideas.

In fact, a symbiotic relationship exists between creativity and self-regulation. To be creative, you must be able to visualize a desired outcome and also to conceive of a plan to achieve it. Both these elements are also essential to self-control. One needs self-control in order to use time wisely, to work diligently, and to have the perseverance to fully develop creative products.

We define self-regulation as: "the ability to get yourself to do (or not do) what you want to do (or not do), when that is difficult." We add the last phrase because you don't need self-control to get yourself to eat ice cream (assuming you like it). And you don't need regulation to get yourself to avoid turnips (assuming you don't like them).

[1] Dacey & Conklin, 2013; Dacey & Lennon, 1998.
[2] e.g., Selman, 2003; Torrance, 2000.
[3] Dacey & Packer, 1992; Dacey & Lennon, 1998.

Students who are good at self-regulation learn better than their peers. For example, they:

- Seek out advice[4] and information.[5]
- Commonly seat themselves toward the front of the classroom.[6]
- Seek out additional resources.[7]
- Voluntarily offer answers to questions.[8]
- Manipulate their learning environments to meet their needs.[9]
- Last but not least, perform better on academic tests and measures of student performance and achievement.[10]

That's quite a list of advantages. Together, they make teaching self-regulation one of the highest priorities of SEL.

ACTIVITY

Control: What Works for You?

Target age: 11 to 15
Goal: To reflect on methods of self-regulation
Materials needed: Paper and pencil or your own electronic device
Script: Suppose you are walking along road on a warm summer day and your stomach is growling. You are SO HUNGRY! However, you realize that the nearest place you can get food is almost a mile in either direction. Even if you run, you know that it's going to be some time before you can satisfy your hunger. You can be miserable until you get to the food, or you can use self-control.

4 Clarebout et al., 2010.
5 DeBruin, Thiede, & Camp, 2011.
6 Labuhn, Zimmerman, & Hasselhorn, 2010.
7 Clarebout, Horz, & Schnotz, 2010.
8 Elstad & Turmo, 2010.
9 Kolovelonis, Goudas, & Dermitzaki, 2011.
10 Schunk & Zimmerman, 2007; Zimmerman, 2008.

How can you manage your feelings so that they don't drive you crazy? What are some techniques you might use to distract yourself from your hunger? On your piece of paper, write down some of these methods that have worked for you in the past. You might also want to ask some of your friends, your teacher, or other adults what they do in these circumstances. After you get through this activity, perhaps you should make a list of the techniques you find useful and memorize them.

Adaptation for younger children: You will probably find that you need to help younger children by suggesting techniques they might use.

Lest you think that self-control is only about social goals, we quote Steven Sosny:

> Research also shows that self-regulation skill is necessary for emotional well-being. Behaviorally, self-regulation is the ability to act in your long-term best interest, consistent with your deepest values. (Violation of one's deepest values causes guilt, shame, and anxiety, which undermine well-being.) Emotionally, self-regulation is the ability to calm yourself down when you're upset and cheer yourself up when you're down. Whether subtle or intense, conscious or unconscious, overt or covert, all emotions have one of three motivations: approach; avoid; and attack.

Let's explore this idea through a couple of activities.

ACTIVITY

 6B

It's about Feelings

Target age: 6 to 10
Goal: To get a better sense of how your child is feeling, and how he is able to control those feelings
Materials needed: Paper and pencil or your own electronic device

Script: Imagine that your teacher has just yelled at you because she thought you made one of your classmates cry, but it wasn't you. When you told her you didn't do it, she wouldn't believe you. How would you feel? What emotions would you have? Write down as many as you can on your paper (don't worry about spelling).

1. _____

2. _____

3. _____

Now let's discuss these feelings. Which ones seem the right ones to you? Which emotions do you wish you didn't have? What can you do about it?

Adaptation for older children: In addition to describing their feelings, older children are often better able to say why they have those feelings and what they think they can do about them.

Delay of Gratification

Delay of gratification refers to postponing an immediate reward for a more desirable one that will take longer or more effort to acquire. Thus it is a component of self-control.

Logue[11] argues that immediate gratification is the same as impulsiveness. An example would be opting to go to the movies with friends rather than studying for an important test happening the next morning. In certain situations, however, there are benefits from acting impulsively, which makes time an important factor in this picture. For example, if your child is invited to go on a spur-of-the-moment camping trip with a friend and his family, it might be a very good idea for you and him to say yes. Self-regulation calls for making good judgments about the pluses and minuses of acting now or delaying for a while. Clearly, however, if you are often unable to make yourself wait to act, you are at a disadvantage.

---

[11] Logue, 1988.

ACTIVITY

I Should Wait, Shouldn't I?

Target age: 11 to 15
Goal: To delay or not to delay—that is the question!
Materials needed: Pencil and paper
Script: In the examples below, which one of the pairs would you pick, A or B?

A	B
1. Five dollars now	1. Seven dollars an hour from now
2. One ticket to a movie now	2. Two tickets to two sports matches in a month
3. Teeth cleaning now	3. Cavity repair a month from now
4. Make up four more pairs of your own.	

Now answer these questions:

- What do your answers say about your style of delay of gratification?
- Are you happy about that?
- If not, what will you do about it?

Adaptation for younger children: The options should be a bit farther apart to make the choice easier. Also, you should offer specific conclusions, such as, "I chose all "now" options. I guess that means I'm not good at waiting. What could I do to get better at it?"

Children progress through two stages in the development of delay of gratification.[12] First, they learn to wait for a more preferred outcome. Then they learn that it is not always advantageous to wait. The two elements that contribute significantly to the development of self-regulation are the ability to estimate time, and the ability to direct attention away from immediate stimuli by, for example, singing a song or playing a game.

---

[12] Sonuga-Barke, 1989.

ACTIVITY

What Do You Think We Should Do?

Age mates discuss when they will give up and get the reward—the longer the wait, the better the reward.
Target age: 6 to 15
Goal: Learn from practicing team self-control
Materials needed: Paper and pencil
Script: Seat your child and two friends or siblings at a table on which you have displayed the choices from Activity 6C (include made-up choices, too).

You and your two friends should discuss with each other the choices each wants to make for each of the options and try to reach agreement on all of them. Each of you should explain his reasons for the decisions he wants your threesome to make. If you can't agree, vote, and the majority wins.

ACTIVITY

Why Should I Wait?

Target age: 11 to 15
Goal: To recognize some of the reasons for delay of gratification
Materials needed: Pencil and paper or your own electronic device
Script: Can you think of any reasons why you should hold off on getting a reward for your behavior? That is, why should you ever delay receiving a prize? Write down your answers to this question, making your list as long as you can.

Adaptation for younger children: (1) Do the activity with only one other child. (2) Tape record and discuss what is said and the points made by each child. (3) Offer smaller prizes.

Locus of Control

"Locus of control" means the extent to which individuals believe they can control the events around them. The concept was developed by Julian Rotter.[13] A person's "locus" (Latin for "place" or "location") is either internal (the person believes he can control his life), or external (he believes his decisions and life are controlled by outside factors or by chance or fate).

Individuals with a strong internal locus of control believe events in their life result primarily from their own actions. For example, when receiving test results, people with an internal locus of control tend to take credit or blame themselves for the grade they got. People with an external locus of control tend to praise or blame external factors, such as the teacher or the test having been too hard.

ACTIVITY

What's an Innie?

Target age: 11 to 15

Goal: To better understand locus of control

Materials needed: Pencil and paper or your own electronic device

Script: As you know from answering the locus of control questions, some people are mainly external. That means they think the control over their lives comes from powers outside them. Others are internal—they think that everything good that happens to them is to their own credit, and that they are to blame for any bad things. They feel they are in complete control of their lives. Many others are in between those two extremes. There are those who take the blame for bad things they do, but not the credit for the good things they achieve. Still others are just the reverse.

For example, there are people who have a deep belief in astrology. This is the idea that everything that happens to us is completely caused by the stars and planets. That is, we are not responsible for what we do—we can't help it. Would you say they are internal or external in terms of locus of control? [They are external.] Can you give me some other examples of people who are likely to be external? [Some answers might be poor people, those who are handicapped mentally or physically, such as being obese, those with low intelligence, and very shy people.] What about some individuals who would be likely to be

[13]   Rotter, 1954.

internal? [Perhaps socially gifted people, those who have high "emotional intelligence," and those who own the best clothes.] Which type of people, internals or externals, is likely to have the most self-control? Why do you say that?

Are you more one way than the other, or are you in the middle? Would you like to know where I think you are on the scale of locus of control?

Adaptation for younger children: You will probably have to explain the terms in this exercise in words your younger child will understand. For example, you may want to substitute "inside people" for the more technically correct term, "internals."

ACTIVITY

I'm an Innie, You're an Outie

Target age: 6 to 10

Goal: To understand how and why people are different in terms of locus of control—a comparison with a friend

Materials needed: Pencil and paper or your own electronic device

Script: As you know, some people are taller than average, and some people are short. Some are very good at solving problems, and other people have a harder time. That's the way it is with self-control. I am going to present you to with some choices, and I want you to write down which of the choices you have selected. In each situation I will describe, you will have five choices. Writing down a 1 means that you are likely to give the same answer as the one I have given you. A number 5 choice means that you would have exactly the opposite answer. And writing down a 3 means that you would be halfway between the two. Let me give you some examples:

If a dentist tells me I have a cavity, my reaction would be:

1. Please, Mom, I really don't need you to come with me on the dental appointment. OR
5. I'm pretty nervous about this. Maybe it would be better if you came with me.

If I fail a test, it would probably be because:

1. I didn't study hard enough. OR
5. The teacher doesn't like me.

Make up some more of your own.

Adaptation for older children: The examples you give will need to be more sophisticated. For example,

1. I love flying—I know the pilot will keep me safe. OR
5. If God had meant us to fly, He would've given us wings.

Risk-Taking

Another factor in self-regulation is risk-taking. Here's an example of what we mean by the term:

In a ring-toss game, ten pegs are set up in a line stretching away from the player. The farther each peg is from the tossing line, the greater the number of points scored for ringing that peg, because the pegs become progressively harder to hit. People who aim at the number 1 peg take a very limited risk, and even if they ring the pin all 10 times, their maximum possible score is 10 (one point per pin = 10 points). Those who aim at the tenth pin have only one-tenth of the likelihood of scoring, so even though the tenth pin is worth 10 points, their most likely score is also 10 (one success = 10 points).

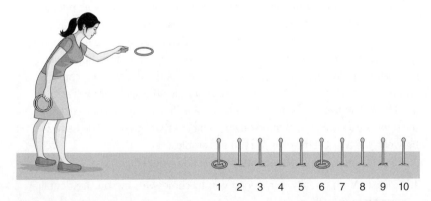

Can you guess which is the most logical pin to try for? Can you say, by doing the math, why that pin is best?

Those willing to take a moderate risk would aim at the fifth or sixth pins. For those two pins, the likely score would be 30 (six successes multiplied by five points for pin #5, and five successes multiplied by six points for pin #6).

Obviously these figures only hold for this particular game, but they are representative of the real world. Those who take tiny risks or huge risks are less likely to be successful than those who take moderate risks. Successful people are those who know how to determine what a moderate risk is, and then confidently take it.

Unfortunately, we parents often discourage sensible risk-taking, and may even cause our children to be risk-averse.[14] A good analogy here is contact with germs. Many parents do all in their power to ensure their children's cleanliness. However, children who live in sterile environments are vulnerable to infection because they do not build up good immunity to infection. Kids *need* to get dirty sometimes. We also need to let them take reasonable risks in other areas of their lives. How do they learn to do this? *Practice.* Only through making judgments can they become aware of how risky things can be, and also how risk can be judged accurately.

What determines a child's risk-taking capacity? To a certain degree, genes. Some children seem to clamor for scary experiences such as riding on a roller coaster. They explore and expand, and when trouble occurs, they may be dazed but are rarely daunted. Other kids are more cautious by nature. Hesitant to venture into unfamiliar territory, they want to preview the script before taking the part. This is why it is so important to support students through inevitable periods of failure or rejection.

ACTIVITY

6H

Should I Dare To Do It?

Target age: 11 to 15
Goal: To become more familiar with risk assessment
Materials needed: Pencil and paper or your own electronic device

---

[14]   Sternberg & Lubart, 1995.

Script: I am going to describe some challenges, and you tell me which ones you would take and why.

A. Bungee jumping
B. Cross the street when the sign says "Don't walk"
C. Rollercoaster riding
D. Gambling at cards
E. Helping a stranger who is looking for his lost puppy
F. Lighting firecrackers
G. Putting down a guessed answer on a test
H. Introducing a friend to a person whose name you're not sure of

Adaptation for younger children: Some of these situations are appropriate (putting down a guessed answer on a test, for instance); others definitely are not (such as lighting firecrackers), and will need to be replaced.

The Shapiro Model—Yielding

Thus far, our definition of self-regulation applies only to the most common type: taking action, also called "assertion." There is another side: turning control over to someone else. This is called "yielding." Both are vital aspects of SEL. Shapiro[15] developed a model of self-control that compares four possible actions:

Shapiro's model of self-control

	Assertion	*Yielding*
Positive		
	1 Active control = positive assertion	2 Passive control = positive yielding
Negative		
	3 Over-control = negative assertion	4 Too little control = negative yielding

The first outcome (#1 above) is the result of active control and positive assertion. An example of this would be planning to work out for an hour per day in order to stay in shape, then sticking to the plan. The second outcome (#2) is the result of relinquishing control and positively yielding to

---

[15] Shapiro et al., 1993.

another. The person in this situation accepts control by another. One example would be allowing a hairdresser or a barber to cut your hair.

The third quadrant (#3) specifies too much control (over-control) combined with a negative assertion. This is the case in which a person exercises an excessive amount of control without taking any positive action. An example would be an eating disorder. Enormous control over one's eating is required, but to negative ends. The final outcome (#4) consists of too little control and negative yielding. An instance might be if you were an alcoholic who refused to go to AA.

ACTIVITY

 61

Letting Mom Be in Charge

Target age: 6 to 10

Goal: To experience how it feels to let you be in charge

Materials needed: Pencil and paper or your own electronic device

Script: The purpose of this activity is to give over control of the decision-making to someone else, and to see how that feels. We need to get four of your friends together so you all can learn how it feels to be in charge.

The first thing you're going to do is to draw lots to determine who will be the "decider." Then, as a group, you're going to try to achieve the following task. [Make up any task that you feel is appropriate for this group. Here is an example.] Your job is to figure out a way that everyone can get across this five-foot circle I have drawn on the ground, without touching the ground. The only things you can use to help you are two four-foot boards.

Here is the solution: Everyone has to follow the leader's directions for the whole task. When the task is complete, have a discussion about how it felt to follow [X's] directions. Discuss whether or not [X] did a good job, and how that made you feel. Did anyone think they could do better job than [X]? Let them try with a new task. Was it frustrating to follow directions even when you didn't want to? What are some situations in which yielding control is necessary? [Examples: being hypnotized, flying on a commercial plane.]

Adaptation for older children: Outward Bound offers many exercises for young teens. Look them up online.

ACTIVITY

Yielding to a Parent's Guidance

Target age: 6 to 15
Goal: To help your child understand clearly the importance of yielding control when you need him to
Materials needed: Activity 2I, Brave Kid
Adapt this activity for any one of your child's fears, explaining to him that you know what you're doing, and that he needs to trust you completely. To the extent that he is able to follow your directions (be sure to take small steps), he will learn that yielding control to a more knowledgeable person is an important part of self-regulation.

Realistic Expectations

By learning to have realistic expectations, your child is more likely to develop self-regulation. He can only learn his limitations by trying to do too much—in a safe environment. For example, most children believe they can stand on one leg with their eyes closed for five minutes. However, few can. Instead of insisting to your child that he can't do it, let him try, but be ready to catch him if necessary. The principle here is that children should be given numerous chances to try out their capacities in safe environments. If they are unlikely to injure themselves, or violate the rights of others, *let them do it*. Experience is the best teacher.

ACTIVITY

Great Expectations

Target age: 6 to 10
Goal: To assist your child to have more accurate evaluations of his own abilities

Materials needed: None

Script: As you know, your weekly allowance is [X]. Suppose I were to give you your entire allowance for the next three months [13 X]. Would you like that? Would you like to have all the money at once so you could buy something expensive? [In our experience, most children will say yes to this.] You need to understand that if you buy something and get tired of it in three weeks, you will have 10 weeks to go before you get your regular allowance. Want to try it?

If your child says no to your offer, ask him why he doesn't think it's a good idea. This should lead to a good discussion of his self-regulation capacity. If he says yes, give him the money and wait to see what happens. Under no circumstances should you give him an advance on his future allowance. In this way, he will get a terrific lesson as to his ability to control his impulses.

Adaptation for older children: There are many variations of this theme for 11- to 16-year-old children. For example, children this age are much better able to anticipate their own behavior. Most are at a stage when they are able to hypothesize about the future. Therefore, before carrying out this experiment, it should be possible to have a really fascinating discussion about your child's self-management abilities.

Scaffolding

Scaffolding is the principle that children can often exceed their normal capacities if they are given a little help. They have the ability to do a task, they just don't realize it. They can reach a higher level of performance with the assistance of a "scaffold." For example a child may believe he cannot do a particular math problem, but if given a tip or two by an age mate, he is surprised to discover that he can reach the solution. By using "How?" and "Why?" questions, you can help your child develop more realistic expectations of himself. As we have said, this contributes greatly to self-regulation. Sometimes a scaffold may only be your words of encouragement: "Try that again. I think you can do it!"

ACTIVITY

Watch and Learn

Target age: 11 to 15
Goal: To assist your child to learn from observing others' decisions
Materials needed: Pencil and paper or your own electronic device
Script: Model "self-talk" to demonstrate how to deal with a difficult decision. For instance, suggest to your child that he tell himself how he is likely to feel if he says yes or no to a temptation.

I want you to watch a friend when she is struggling with her cravings, such as whether or not to eat ice cream just before dinner time. Write down what you are observing, including what she says. You should then note the implications of her decision as you see them, and perhaps ask her what she thinks they are. For example, you might say, "Jane wants to eat candy very badly, even though she knows to would keep her from wanting to eat vegetables. Waiting is hard work sometimes!" In this case, both you and Jane are offering a scaffold for your child's effort to understand techniques of self-control. As with the other principles in this chapter, nothing succeeds like opportunities to practice and evaluate efforts to gain self-regulation.

Adaptation for younger children: You will probably need to suggest what you think your child should be observing. Also, you may want him to record his observations as it may take too long to write them down as he is also watching his friend's deliberations.

ACTIVITY

The Buddy System

Target age: 11 to 16
Goal: Learn to share goals with another person, especially with a reward strategy

Materials needed: A running track

Script: When someone helps you to achieve your goals, we call it "scaffolding." They support you as you try to go higher. You are using scaffolding when you ask someone to only give you your reward if you reach your ultimate goal. Such a person is known as your "buddy." Let's suppose that you want to run around a quarter-mile track 12 times, for a total of three miles. Let's also suppose you decided to give yourself three dollars from your savings if you reach that goal.

If you're like most people, and you get tired after eight laps, you will be tempted to decide that it's good enough and you will want to reward yourself right then and there. This is where buddy comes in. Your buddy watches you run, and gets to keep the three dollars if you don't do the entire twelve rounds. Thus you will be highly motivated to achieve your goal.

Adaptation for younger children: The principle of the buddy system, as well as scaffolding, is the same for younger children. The goal, however, has to be more easily achieved.

Homework

For many children, doing homework becomes an emotionally charged event and one of the most disgruntling aspects of school life. It is surely one of the central tests of a child's self-management! In a study of nearly 2,000 secondary school students, Xu found that "Doing well on homework is related to teacher feedback, peer-oriented reasons for doing homework, arranging the environment, managing time, and monitoring motivation."[16] Girls tend to be better at homework and other types of self-regulation than boys, probably because it is such a part of their gender role in most societies. Girls are more likely to use cognitive imagery to control their emotions (e.g., sitting beside a lovely lake), whereas boys use physical means (e.g., muscle tension).[17] Apparently cognitive trumps physical in terms of self-regulation.

In Chapter 2, on character formation, we talked about defense mechanisms. One of the most common is called "repression." This refers to our tendency to forget unpleasant responsibilities. Can you think of a better example than doing homework?

---

[16] Xu, 2011.
[17] Dacey, deSalvatore, & Robinson, 1997.

ACTIVITY

Don't Forget

Target age: 6 to 15

Goal: For your child to remember to do homework without you "hucking" him

Materials needed: 3″ × 5″ cards, felt tip pen, tape

Script: The defense mechanism known as "repression" refers to an unconscious way people have of forgetting to do things we would rather not do.

Do you want to do your homework every day? Maybe not, but what a pain it is to have to make up for skipping it, such as staying after school, extra work, and the like. It's better just to get it done, isn't it? The way to overcome the temptation to forget about doing homework is to provide yourself with unavoidable reminders that you *want* to do this task. When you put notes up on the wall or a mirror and you look at them every day, they're a constant reminder of something you want to achieve. I think in the long run, you'll be glad you did!

Fluency and Flexibility of Self-Control Strategies

As you will see in Chapter 11, on creative thinking, fluency refers to the number of possible solutions a person can think of for a problem: the higher the *number of ideas*, the greater the fluency. Flexibility results when the *types* of solutions a person dreams up are significantly different from each other. Both of these factors figure powerfully in a person's ability to be imaginative. This is also true when it comes to self-regulation. The more you can anticipate all the possible consequences of your behavior (fluency), the better able you are to control yourself. The better you can see the differences between them (flexibility), the more likely you are to have control. Being able to spot different kinds of implications makes you an even better self-manager.

Not surprisingly, because younger kids have a smaller repertoire of strategies, we expect them to have less self-control.[18] Also, children who are high

---

[18]   Cleary & Chen, 2009.

in intellectual curiosity are more apt to anticipate the outcomes of their behavior.[19] Both of these variables tend to encourage better self-management because they are associated with fluency and flexibility.

ACTIVITY

So You Want to Quit?

Target age: 6 to 10

Goal: To develop the skills of fluency and flexibility in self-regulation

Materials needed: Pencil and paper or your own electronic device

Script: Imagine that you are a nail-biter, and you really want to stop doing it. Or you could choose some other pattern that you want to get rid of. Try to pick some habit of yours you really hate.

Now let's talk about what you could do to change the pattern. I want you to keep going until your list of solutions yields at least five methods, such as painting your nails with something that tastes bad. I also want you to try your best to make each item on your list of five really different from each other. For example, you could add wearing gloves to try to get yourself to stop. I'll give you those two ideas. Now you try to think of three more that are unlike each other. And if you do, your reward will be [X]!

Adaptation for older children: The total number of ideas must equal seven. Children in this age group should probably come up with their own problem, and should get a bigger reward, especially if your older child actually carries out one of the plans.

When to Withdraw Support

The goal of all education, whether we are teachers or parents, is to make it unnecessary for us always to be present. That is, we want self-regulation to become engrained in everyday behavior. Thus we need to think about how and when to fade the support our children need to achieve mastery.

---

[19] Wang & Holcombe, 2010.

You will need to be on the lookout for signs that your child has internalized self-regulation. Unfortunately, we cannot be specific in our advice on how to do this, because there is so much variation in a child's capacity for it. Age, gender, self-confidence, creativity, sensitivity, intelligence, and maturity are all factors that must be considered. What we can say is that you need to be on the lookout for opportunities to *offer practice*, to *model the skills*, and to *reward self-mastery*. Parents who understand that these are their goals almost always do a fine job of it.

Part III
Social Awareness

7

Competing and Cooperating

"Too many youth athletes get over-focused on getting the win," says Scott Goldman. "I tell our athletes all the time, if you just want to win, go play against a 4th grader. But if you want your win to have meaning, play against someone who can beat you. I would add this: you learn and grow much more from losses than wins. The losses build your resilience, your adaptability, your ability to get up after being kicked in the stomach, literally or metaphorically.[1]

Competition is everywhere. We are constantly being encouraged to compare ourselves to others. In fact, evolution has programmed it into our genes.[2] Schools are rated on their test scores, colleges on their graduates' success, teams on their win/loss records. Employees are rewarded with higher salaries and promotions, beauty pageant contestants by winning Miss Whatever (or the always dreaded Miss Congeniality).

Even when competition is not formal, it is present. Children compare toys and lunches. Teens compare everything: who is most popular, has the best clothes, is smartest, or the best athlete. Parents worry, is my child doing

[1]   Brunner, 2014.
[2]   Das, 2013.

Your Child's Social and Emotional Well-Being: A Complete Guide for Parents and Those Who Help Them, First Edition. John S. Dacey, Lisa B. Fiore, and Steven Brion-Meisels.
© 2016 John Wiley & Sons, Ltd. Published 2016 by John Wiley & Sons, Ltd.
Companion website: www.wiley.com/go/daceywellbeing

as well as their child? Even elders compare themselves: am I as fit as my neighbor down the block? Like all of us, our children and grandchildren need to compete well and ethically.

Although cooperation is often less visible, it is actually more important to our lives than competition. Most of us enjoy working well with others more than competing with them. Research in education suggests that students do better individually when they work cooperatively.[3] Employers know that a good team member is an invaluable asset. They can teach a new employee how to program the computer but it is much more difficult to teach her the skills of cooperation—or many other SEL skills, for that matter.[4] Research in evolution and biology suggests that the human species has done so well because we know how to cooperate. Far from "survival of the fittest," the human story could be titled "survival of the most connected." This is true for families, neighborhoods, and nations as well as the human species in general.[5]

How do we decide when to compete and when to cooperate? There are, of course, no easy answers to that question, but there are some guidelines. And SEL can help.

Competition, Cooperation, and CASEL

Cooperation and competition have been identified by CASEL,[6] as well as by social theorists, as essential developmental skills and attitudes. Here some examples of how they are woven into CASEL's five core elements:

- *Self-awareness.* Self-awareness is shaped by competition and cooperation: we understand our skills when we interact with others. We might think we are great at chess or baseball, but then we encounter someone who has stronger skills. A string of losses or poor grades can make a child think she is not worthy, or is dumb or lazy—whereas a string of wins or good grades can help her see herself as capable and worthy of praise. Research suggests that cooperative activities help strengthen positive self-awareness—and perhaps as importantly, a sense that you

---

[3] Cohen, 2011; Johnson, Johnson, & Stamme, 2000; Slavin, 2011.
[4] Johnson, Johnson and Holubec, 1998; Selman, 2003, 2012; Weissbourd, 2009.
[5] Rifkin, 2009.
[6] CASEL, 2014.

can use your skills to help others. Competitive activities can do this for a few (the winners), with significant damage to the many (the losers).[7]

- *Self-management.* Self-management is also entwined with competition and losing. Successful cooperation requires self-management. We can't always have it "my way." We can't all be leaders. We need to share our ideas and take turns. We need to manage our anger when a team mate or group member falls short of our expectations.

    Competition also involves self-management. When we win, do we gloat or boast, or do we congratulate our opponent? When we lose do we fly off the handle? Our ability to manage our emotions almost always affects the ways in which we compete (or cooperate) in the future.

- *Social awareness.* The great basketball competitors Larry Bird and Magic Johnson both say their greatest pleasure in the game involved their respect for the other. Taking the perspective of others can help us win. Social awareness is the key to working together to win.

- *Relationship skills.* Positive relationships can be strengthened through healthy, fair competition. But competition can also damage those bonds. Cooperation always strengthens healthy affiliations. Even an unsuccessful cooperative effort can become an opportunity for learning.

- *Responsible decision-making.* Although it is sometimes more time-consuming, making decisions cooperatively has proven consistently to lead to better decisions.[8] Responsible decision-making involves many cooperative skills: listening, sharing ideas, respecting divergent perspectives, looking for common ground, identifying win-win solutions—and creating a plan to act on our decisions.

Clearly there are situations in which competition provides the best solution to a problem, and many other situations in which cooperation is best. Therefore in the next three sections, we suggest strategies for achieving each.

Activities that Foster Better Competition

When administrators, coaches, parents, and fans understand competition and are committed to helping children get the most from their competitive experiences, it is viewed almost universally as positive. However, when members of any of

---

[7] Johnson & Johnson, 2014.
[8] Tencati & Zsolnai, 2009.

these important adult groups, particularly coaches, lose perspective and fail to put the child's welfare first, competition can become a negative experience.[9]

The first rule in competition is the "Goldilocks rule." A person's competitors must not be substantially better or worse at an activity than she is. If they are more highly skilled, your child will give up. If they are less skilled, your child will get bored. The match should be "just right." Our first activity helps children to enter only the right competitions for them.

ACTIVITY

Goldilocks Games

Target age: 6 to 15

Goal: To help your child know her abilities objectively

Materials needed: The table provided below

Script: If you just want to win, go play against a kindergartner! But that wouldn't be much fun, would it? The same would be true for competing with a high school kid, right? For each of the activities of this questionnaire, I would like you to check the box next to it that best describes you: below average, average, above average. I am also going rate you to as to how skilled I think you are in each of these activities, too. Okay, let's get started.

Data recording sheet

Activity	Above average	Average	Below average	Agree/disagree
Writing				
Math				
Running speed				
Strength				
Good manners				
Reliability				
Honesty				

---

[9]   Burton & Raedeke, 2014.

On the blank rows, add any abilities you and your child also would like to rate.

Now let's see what ratings you and I agree on, and which ones we disagree about. Let's talk about the ones in which we each rated you differently. What's the best way for us to figure out which one of us was right? What's the best way to use this information when you are deciding which competitions to enter?

ACTIVITY

Becoming a Better Sport

Target age: 6 to 10
Goal: To help your child gain control over her feelings when competing

Did you ever meet anyone who is just naturally a good sport? Individuals who never get mad when they lose, at other people or at themselves? Neither have we! This is probably because of the Dunning–Kruger effect,[10] which is "the tendency of unskilled individuals to exaggerate their abilities."

For this activity, you should try to engage at least four children, but the more the merrier. They do not have to be of exactly the same age, but their ages should be similar. Divide the children into two equal groups, with one group sitting to your left and one group sitting to your right.
Materials needed: A set of 10 questions that can easily be answered by the age group you have chosen. For example, if the children are 7-year-olds, some sample questions might be:

1. "What day is it today?"
2. "How many kids are in your group?"
3. "What's my age?"

[10] Wikipedia, 2014.

Script: Okay, children, this is how this game will work: I will ask a question of the children on my left. If they get the correct answer, they get one point. If they don't, I will ask the group on my right, and if they get the correct answer, they will get two points. Ready?

Begin asking your questions, and keep a record of the score of the group on the left. You can be confident that, pretty soon, the group on the right will start to complain: "Hey, that's not fair!" "The questions you're giving them are too easy!" "They're cheating, we don't have a chance!" "Why should you treat them as special—there is nothing special about them!" Now say to the children on the right,

"Okay, you are correct, this game was not fair. You never had a chance to score points because the questions were too easy and the other group got all of them right. I can understand why you got upset. However, suppose you were trying to be good sports about it. What would you have said instead?"

The children will probably say things like, "Congratulations, you won!" or "You guys did a nice job. Well done!" Now ask the group who won the contest,

"How did it feel when someone accused you of being cheaters?""Was it better when they said, 'Nice job,' even though you knew you only won because the questions were so easy?"

[Be sure to give them plenty of time to answer.]

Good sports are people who keep control of their feelings and try never to say mean things if they lose. As I said, this contest wasn't fair, but the losing group members weren't exactly being good sports, now, were they? Let's think of some things that you could say when you lose a real contest, things that will make the winners feel good about you. I will write the list down for you and you can copy it. In the future, when we play a game or have some kind of contest, I would like you to practice these words or phrases, and I hope you will try really hard to use them, even if you feel sad about losing.

Adaptation for older children:

- Make the questions harder, but not so hard that they don't get almost all of them right.
- Ask the youth to define "good sport."
- Discuss when we ought to try to be good sports, and when we should disagree with the rules of the game.
- Ask the youth to give examples of times when they have been a good sport.
- Ask them to explain why they think they were.

Activities that Foster Better Cooperation

Here are a few specific guidelines that will promote cooperation:

- *Invite children to help.* Often children want to help but they are not asked. A child helper can sometimes cause more work—more clean-up, more organization, more everything! But engaging children in real helping activities early on teaches important SEL skills.
- *Model cooperation every chance you get.* Children learn by watching. So the best teaching we do is to *show* what we want our children to learn. For instance, try to resolve your spousal disagreements privately, so your children will tend to observe cooperation between you.
- *Appreciate acts of cooperation.* Consistently notice cooperative behaviors—and say something.
- *Play cooperative games.* Although most commercial games are competitive, there are cooperative games on the market (see our website: www.wiley.com/go/daceywell being). Cooperative games are increasingly popular in after-school, church, and community settings. You can also modify competitive games so that they are cooperative, as you will see below.
- *Read and discuss stories, films, and TV programs about cooperation.* Many children's stories include themes of cooperation, at all ages. All PBS series like *Curious George, Arthur* or *Sesame Street* often emphasize themes of cooperation. Pixar films show cross-generational cooperation in the film *Up*, and cross-cultural cooperation (among penguins) in *Happy Feet*.
- *Don't be afraid of competition.* Winning and losing well are important social/emotional skills. If your child or grandchild returns from a particularly difficult encounter with losing, you can use the experience as a learning opportunity.

ACTIVITY

You Build What I Build

Target age: 6 to 10

Goal: To develop core skills of communication and perspective-taking, and sometimes conflict resolution as well

Materials needed: Two identical sets of children's blocks—about six to eight in each set. The blocks should include a range of shapes and colors: triangle, rectangle, cylinder, cube, etc. You will also need one large piece of cardboard, cloth, or paper (about 2 × 3 feet) to serve as a mission barrier. You can play this effectively with two or more children.

Script: The barrier separates the two players (or teams of players). Each individual or team has the same set of blocks—e.g., two rectangles, one triangle, two cubes, one bridge shape. One individual or team builds a simple structure using their five pieces. They then need to instruct the other individual or team to build exactly the same structure. The "instructors" must use ONLY their voices; the "builders" will not see the structure until the end. The instructors can't show pieces or use their hands to indicate placement; they can ONLY use words. The copying team can ask questions. When they think the task is done, the wall can be removed.

As you can see, this game offers opportunities for learning how to cooperate (instructor with builder, within and between teams). Then the questions begin.

- *What?* What did we do? Was it fun? Frustrating? Both?
- *Now what?* What skills did you use? [examples: listening, giving clear communications, thinking about a second perspective, following instructions, asking questions, communicating only with words, being flexible, etc.]
- *So what?* How do these skills help us in real life? In the classroom? On the playground? Within the family? How does communication cause conflict? How can we take the perspective of others in our family or classroom? What gets in the way of successful communication? How can we make it better when communication has broken down?

Adaptation for older children:

- Use double the number of blocks.
- Use double the variety of blocks.
- Use attribute blocks instead of shape blocks.
- Allow less time for questions.

ACTIVITY

7D

Look, Mom, No Hands!

Target age: 11 to 15

Goal: Develop interpersonal cooperation skills

Materials needed: Six paper cups (6-ounce or larger). One rubber band with four "handles" attached to it. The handles are pieces of string (or yarn) 6 inches long. The structure looks like a ring (rubber band) with four branches (strings)—or a spider web with four filaments. Here is a drawing of it:

Script: Your goal is to create a tower with these six upside-down paper cups: three on the first level, two on the second, and one on the third. However, you can ONLY use the rubber band tool and can NOT use words. You must coordinate your work silently. Each of you pulls on a string until the rubber band is stretched enough to fit over a cup. [Note: If a cup turns over or rolls off the table, participants can pick it up and place it back on the table. Other than that, no touching!] If you succeed quickly, you can create variations: add more cups, turn the top cup upside down, set a time limit, etc.

- *Now*, how well were you able to communicate with each other? What was fun? What was frustrating? How did we do as a team?
- *Now what?* What skills did we need in order to succeed? [Examples include non-verbal communication, coordination, patience, willingness to follow a leader, maybe even prior planning.] How did you manage to communicate so you could work together?
- *So what?* How do these skills help us get along or succeed in life? In our family? Our classroom or school? When have we shown leadership that includes others? When have we shown a kind of "bully" leadership—"My way or the highway"? How does this kind of activity cause conflict? How is it like other activities that can cause conflict? Can you tell me how you think we can work with conflict in the future?

Adaptation for younger children: Even quite young children can learn to manipulate the strings tied to the rubber band so as to pick up and move the cups. Of course it is harder for them to work the rig as a foursome, so you may have to offer some instruction. The biggest difference, however, is in the level of sophistication in the questions you ask. You will have to experiment with the level of questions they can handle well, but we know they can learn quite a bit from the experience.

ACTIVITY

7E

Don't Goof Up!

Target age: 6 to 15
Goal: Most children view the game of Pick-Up-Sticks or Jenga as having one winner with everyone else being losers. Played collaboratively, several cooperative skills are learned

Materials needed: Pick-Up-Sticks or Jenga stacking blocks. A minimum of two players

Script: This game of [Pick-Up-Sticks or Jenga] is usually played against an opponent. The goal in each of these games is to take turns moving a piece without disturbing any of the others. You try to pick the easy choices, so your challenger has a harder choice to make. This time, you and your friends are going to play it a little differently.

You will each be a partner. You can discuss each move together, with the goal being the same: move as many pieces as the two of you can without disturbing any of the others. You can play several times, trying to increase your last score. Before you begin, talk about your strategy. How can you cooperate to get a really high score?

When you have played several games, answer this question: What have you learned about cooperating, and how can you apply these lessons to real life?

Activities that Foster Cooperation *and* Competition

ACTIVITY

7F

Your Achievement Style

Target age: 11 to 15

Goal: to discern your child's preferred mode of achievement—competitive or cooperative

Materials needed: A copy of the questionnaire below

Script: I would like you to read the statements on this questionnaire. Then I would like you to put an X in the box that best reflects how *you* feel about the statement. For example, if you agree with a statement, put an X in the *Agree* box that follows it. When you're done we will score the results.

Achievement style recorder sheet

#	Statement	Strongly agree	Agree	Disagree	Strongly disagree	Total for each question	Score for competition	Score for cooperation
1	You're good at solving problems because you tend to get answers faster than others.*							
2	You have built a network of close friends.							
3	Usually, you're a leader.*							
4	When someone challenges you, you look for ways to complement each other.							
5	Challenges from others make you anxious.							
6	You like it best when everyone succeeds.							
7	You believe you're better off working alone.*							
8	You always strive to be the best in your class.*							
9	You don't like it when somebody tries to persuade you to do something their way.							
10	You think winning is always to be preferred to losing.*							
	Total Score							

First, score this questionnaire for each question (in the "Total for each question" column) by giving yourself four points if you strongly agree, three points if you agree, two points if you disagree, and one point if you strongly disagree.

Next, add up your total points for each of two groups of questions. The first group is for how competitive you tend to be. You should total your score for the following five questions: numbers 1, 3, 7, 8, and 10. These questions have an asterisk after the statement. Enter your scores in the next-to-last column ("Score for competition"). Put the total in the bottom of that column.

Next, add up your total points for the second group of questions, which is for how cooperative you tend to be. You should total your score the following five questions: numbers 2, 4, 5, 6, and 9. They do not have an asterisk after the statement. Enter your scores in the last column ("Score for cooperation"). Put the total in the bottom of that column.

If you got a score above 10 on competition, that indicates that you like a contest when you seek to achieve your goals. If you got a score above 10 on cooperation, that indicates that you prefer to work collaboratively with others to achieve your goals. If your total scores on both types were above 10, it may mean that you are an extrovert with strong incentives to reach your objectives. If you total scores on both types was below 10, it may mean that you are an introvert, a shy person who is not so highly motivated.

How do you feel about your two scores? If yours show you to be a competitor, do you think being a collaborator would be better? Or if yours show you to be a collaborator, do you think being a competitor would be better? If you are not happy about the scores you got, what could you do to change them?

Allow your child to think of strategies for change. Two possible strategies would be to:

- Try to be more intentional when seeking to achieve your goals. Think twice before acting.
- Look again at the 10 questions for clues about what to try to change.

Adaptations for younger children: Read each question to your child and explain its meaning to her.

ACTIVITY

Working with Your Child's School

Fifty years ago, noted sociologist James Coleman was looking out the window of his University of Chicago classroom, from which he could see the football team doing calisthenics. It was a cold, rainy November afternoon, but most of the young men were smiling or laughing, and all seemed to be enthusiastic. "How could we possibly attain that kind of motivation throughout a child's education?" he wondered. "What makes playing a game such as football so much more valuable to the youth than classroom work?"

In a flash, the answer came to him. The youth were so fervent for two reasons:

- There is great joy in working together as a team for a common goal.
- The common goal is to win in competition against other teams.

Why couldn't the same simple formula be used to improve learning in all subjects, at almost any grade level? Wouldn't the use of these two principles also empower teachers as well as students? For children, the competition could be between groups in the classroom. For older youth, it could be intra- or intermural.

As you undoubtedly know, Coleman's imaginative concept has not been adopted in most schools. There are numerous reasons for this, but we believe it still has excellent potential. Perhaps you might like to lobby your child's teachers or principal to give the idea a try.

Let's suppose you love the idea of your child's teachers or principal establishing such a plan. Nevertheless, students would need careful coaching on how to work together to prepare for such a competition. The materials used for testing each team's skills would need to be carefully designed, and evaluation techniques must be seen as fair. If such a scheme were attempted at your child's school, however, opportunities for fostering high-quality cooperation and competition would abound. SEL really would be happening.

8

Neither Being Bullied nor Being a Bully

"Welcome home!" said her mother.
"Welcome home!" said her father.
"School is no place for me," said Chrysanthemum. "They said I even
look *like a flower. They pretended to pick me and smell me."*
"Oh, pish," said her mother. "They're just jealous."
"And envious and begrudging and discontented and jaundiced,"
said her father.
"Who wouldn't be jealous of a name like yours?" said her mother.
"After all, it's absolutely perfect," said her father.[1]

Bullying is a familiar topic to most parents, children, or teachers, as the story that opened this book implies. The American Academy of Child and Adolescent Psychiatry states that "close to half of all children will experience school bullying at some point while they are at primary or secondary school."[2] Many others, obviously, will do the bullying. What can a parent or teacher do to help break the cycle of bullying? And how can adults help children avoid participating in the cycle?

[1]   Henkes, 1991, p. 18
[2]   AACAP, 2011.

Your Child's Social and Emotional Well-Being: A Complete Guide for Parents and Those Who Help Them, First Edition. John S. Dacey, Lisa B. Fiore, and Steven Brion-Meisels.
© 2016 John Wiley & Sons, Ltd. Published 2016 by John Wiley & Sons, Ltd.
Companion website: www.wiley.com/go/daceywellbeing

Many organizations have developed precisely because of the shared concern and desire for action to protect children from bullying. Moms Fight Back, an organization dedicated to empowering mothers on behalf of their children, has analyzed the quality of anti-bullying legislation in each state, and assigned grades based on the quality of programs designed to eradicate bullying in a systematic way, with support from the government.[3]

While legislation is absolutely critical to enforce policies that will affect children, it's sometimes difficult to identify the players in the bullying cycle. The terms "bully," "victim," and "bystander" are commonly used to describe what takes place. Researchers note that many bullies have been victims of bullying themselves. More discrete categories and definitions have evolved to distinguish specific attributes of bullies, victims, and bystanders:[4]

- *Aggressive bullies.* The most common type of bully, they tend to be physically strong, quick-tempered, exhibit little fear, have the ability to convince and/or dominate others, and display little or no empathy for others. They are typically motivated by desire for power and domination. Aggressive bullies are often popular in earlier school years, and lose their status as peers begin to develop their own critical thinking abilities.
- *Passive bullies.* They do not initiate bullying incidents but are quick to join in when something is underway. They typically have low self-esteem, tend to lack confidence, and have many challenges in their home environments. Passive bullies often side with aggressive bullies, displaying fierce loyalty to these allies.
- *Bully-victims.* They have been on the receiving end of bullying as victims, and turn to bullying others who are less physically strong than themselves. Bully-victims are more often diagnosed with anxiety and depression than other types of bullies.
- *Passive victims.* These represent the largest proportion of victimized children. They are perceived as weak, fearful, and withdrawn by their peers, and typically have few close friends. These qualities make them easy targets for aggressive bullies. Passive victims' responses to bullying tend to change over time. While they might at first cry or become angry, as they get older they may avoid bullying situations by skipping school or, in extreme cases, leaving home.

[3]   See http://momsfightback.org/united-states-bullying-report-card-2014/.
[4]   Olweus, 1978.

- *False victims.* These individuals typically complain about being victimized in an attempt to gain attention from others. There is a tendency for children who demonstrate such behavior to elicit a negative response from adults, similar to a "boy who cried wolf" situation where people turn a deaf ear because false claims have been made too often.
- *Provocative victims.* These children tend to behave in ways that elicit negative behaviors from peers, such as anger, frustration, and irritation. These individuals are prone to classroom disruption because of their behavior, as it is often difficult for them to remain on-task. Provocative victims sometimes display qualities of aggressive bullies (e.g., hostility) and passive victims (e.g., low self-esteem).
- *Bystanders.* They aren't necessarily targets of bullies' attention, but tend to be eager to witness bullying. They choose not to help victims or report incidents for fear of their own safety.

In recent years there has also been a tendency to classify bullying incidents into "traditional" and "cyber" forms.[5] Traditional bullying involves incidents that occur in person, which may be of a physical or verbal nature, and always have a social element. Cyberbullying involves incidents that occur digitally or electronically—not in person (e.g., online)—and therefore the bully is often able to remain anonymous. Examples of cyberbullying may include social media forums on the Internet, cell phone, or texting exchanges, and other media outlets.

There are numerous factors that contribute to bullying. These include the motivation of the bully, the availability and characteristics of the victim, and the context in which the bullying occurs. Consequences of bullying include depression and anxiety—on the part of bullies, victims, and bystanders alike.

In an attempt to break the bullying cycle, schools and other organizations have developed programs that address bullying and the underlying currents that sustain the bullying culture. For example, since evidence shows that mindfulness interrupts one's stream of negative thoughts, many anti-bullying programs teach meditation and breathing exercises.[6] However, some recent research has indicated that students in schools with anti-bullying programs are more likely to be bullied than students in schools with no anti-bullying programs.[7] It may be that many schools where bullying prevails do have programs, but they aren't powerful enough to make much of a dent in the bullying.

---

[5]　Boulton et al., 2014, p. 1.
[6]　Flannick, 2014
[7]　Trowbridge, 2013

One high school student shared her opinion in a recent *Huffington Post Teen* online article, stating, "Up until now, our society has been trying to reform bullies while treating victims as martyrs. By focusing on bullies, we have actually given them more power. Instead, we need to shift our focus away from bullying behaviors and concentrate on building the inner strength of all students."[8] What an argument for SEL!

Conflict resolution, trust-building, encouraging group identity and therefore responsibility for others, and cooperation and competition are but a few of the complex strategies now being attempted. Efforts to increase students' self-esteem affect bullies, victims, and bystanders alike. Successful anti-bullying typically attempts to build greater capacity for empathy. As was discussed in Chapter 3, mindfulness practices (e.g., meditation, centering) encourage connectedness and perspective-taking, and also improve concentration. Mindfulness practices foster values that are more empathetic. The following activities are designed to enhance your child's capacity for empathy, and to encourage positive interactions with others.

Activities that Promote Empathy

ACTIVITY

Mirror, Mirror

Target age: 6 to 15
Goal: To help your child to recognize that his own impulses and reactions are different from those of someone else
Materials needed: None
Script: Invite your child and several others to stand facing each other. If you are practicing this exercise with one child, then you can face your child in the "mirror" position. Designate which children will be the actors and which will be the mirrors.

---

[8]   Baird, 2014

Let's begin the mirror activity. Picture a mirror you have seen somewhere before. What happens when you look in the mirror? What do you see?

A mirror shows us our reflection—it shows us what we look like, and any movement we make is copied in the reflection. Face your partners—now, those of you who are the actors will start to make movements, especially facial expressions, when I signal you. Those of you who are the mirrors will copy your partners' moves as well as you can. You will need to stare at your partner, and notice his movements, big and small—even tiny! [Partners mirror each other for two to three minutes. Encourage the children to use their whole bodies, including facial expressions, jumping, or other moves.]

Now let's switch, and the movers will be the mirrors. The mirrors will copy the movers' actions. [Allow two to three minutes for this.]

OK, let's talk about what just happened. Was it more fun for you to be an actor or a mirror? What did you like about being an actor? A mirror? What is difficult about being an actor or leader, and what is easy? What is difficult about being a mirror or follower, and what is easy? How can noticing what other kids are doing be helpful to you?

Adaptation for older children: Older children can imagine real situations in which mirroring could be used. Also, they can decide whether they want to be actors or followers.

ACTIVITY

 8B

Trust Walk

Target age: 11 to 15
Goal: To help children experience vulnerability in a safe, controlled environment
Materials needed: A blindfold, bandana or scarf. This experience also works best with several children
Script: Invite several of your child's age mates to pair up. If you are practicing this exercise with one child, then you and the child can be partners. Ask the children to decide who will be the first with his eyes closed, and who will be the guide.

We're going to take a walk together. On this walk, one person will have his eyes covered, and one person will be the guide. It is the guide's job to make sure that the person with his eyes blinded is safe. This means making sure that no one bumps into anything, trips over anything, or falls or stubs their toes. When you are the guide, you should make the walk as interesting as possible for your partner—you may go up or down stairs, and enter rooms with different sounds or smells. As you're walking, touch different objects or feel different textures on the walls or floors.

Take this trust walk without anyone speaking. Try to be silent the entire time. Use your imagination only. When I tell you, you will stop wherever you are and switch roles—the guides will put on the blindfolds and those who were blindfolded will now be the guides.

When the children have completed their turns as guides and trusting, blindfolded partner, you may discuss some or all of the following questions:

- How did it feel to have your eyes closed and to rely on your partner?
- Did you feel more comfortable blindfolded or as the guide?
- Did you enjoy the trust walk? What did you like most about it? What would you change next time?
- How has doing this activity changed you for the better? For example, do you feel more trusting of each other?

Adaptation for younger children: You might start this activity with a discussion about what the word trust actually means. For example, how do you know whether or not you can count on someone?

ACTIVITY

8C

On a Desert Island I Would Bring...

Target age: 11 to 15
Goal: To help children recognize different strengths in others and how they might better appreciate those strengths

Materials needed: Index cards or small pieces of paper to write on; pencils
Script: We're going to pretend that you're heading to a desert island for a short stay. If you could have one person travel with you, who would you like to be there with you? What kind of person would be most helpful? Write your answers on your index card/piece of paper.

Ask your child to share his answers. For example, he might say, "I want someone who knows how to cook" or he might say, "I would want someone funny to make me laugh while we're there." As your child shares the kinds of people that would be most desirable, see if you can notice themes or gaps that present themselves. For example, did your child say he'd want someone who's a really good sports player to be there? Many skills and qualities that are valued in some circumstances and social circles will likely be less important on a desert island. You might have a conversation about why it's so important that people have different strengths and talents, and that all over the world these are valued in different ways. Try to draw the link from being different to being bullied.

Adaptation for younger children: The depth of insight of younger children will probably be different, but they too will benefit from realizing that people with different strengths from their own would be most helpful in any isolated situation.

Conflict Resolution and Negotiation

All incidents of bullying involve interpersonal conflict, whether person-to-person or through the use of electronic contact. Children should not come to view all conflict as bad, however. On the contrary, conflicts between people are inevitable. It is more empowering for children to learn to be respectful of another person's needs and ideas, and not to view differences of opinion as threatening, dangerous, or hostile. When they learn to resolve conflicts successfully, the good–bad, win–lose dichotomies dissolve. The bases for healthy, long-term relationships are established. The following activities are designed to stimulate children's thinking about conflict and to help them establish a repertoire of successful negotiation strategies.

ACTIVITY

Inner Conflicts

Target age: 6 to 15

Goal: To help your child recognize internal conflicts that he may be experiencing, and to notice how they affect him and others

Materials needed: Conflicts sheets (see Activity 8E below); pencils, crayons, colored pencils for drawing

Script: Think about what choices you have made recently—today, yesterday, this week, or even this month. Choices are sometimes complicated, and sometimes they are quite simple. Maybe you chose what flavor yogurt to eat for lunch, or what television show to watch. Maybe you chose which friend to invite to come over, or which relatives to invite to a holiday party.

Sometimes when we make a decision, we feel conflicted about it—we aren't sure if it's right. Maybe there is no right or wrong answer at all! We sometimes find ourselves thinking about whether a choice that we make is in sync with our values, about how we think we are supposed to act. Using the conflict sheet, write down some conflicts that you've had. Do you feel good about each decision you made? How have your choices affected you? How do your choices affect others?

Do your best to provoke as much discussion about the subject as you can.

ACTIVITY

Conflict Strips

Target age: 11 to 15

Goal: To help your child explore conflict and how it presents opportunities for improvement

Materials needed: Sheets of paper, preferably white or light-colored, folded into eighths; sample comic strips cut out of the newspaper; markers, crayons, and/or colored pencils for drawing. A familiar children's story or fable, such as *The Fox and the Sour Grapes* or *The Wizard of Oz* can be helpful to get ideas flowing or as discussion starters.

Script: Let's think about a familiar story where the characters got into some sort of conflict. How do you think they are feeling? How can you tell? Have you experienced a feeling of struggle recently? Using the paper you have in front of you, think about how you would draw the conflict you felt. Try to use all eight of the folded panels of this paper, showing the stages through which the problem progressed. Or, you might want to represent the encounter by clipping sections from these comic strips. What scene would go in each of the eight sections?

When your child is finished drawing, ask him to tell you about the conflict strip.

Why did you draw what you did? How did the conflict come out? Are there any aspects of the conflict strip that you would change, if you could? See if you can think of some possible alternate endings.

Adaptation for younger children: Other stories might be appropriate, such as *Three Little Pigs*. Also, younger children may use sheets of paper folded into fourths.

Activities that Promote Positive Group Interaction

While blatant forms of bullying and mistreatment are obvious (e.g., taking a student's lunch money), for children in groups, more subtle forms of mistreatment (e.g., shunning) can be as devastating. These understated forms of bullying often tend to occur in smaller schools, or in classrooms with fewer children. Such opportunities for exclusion from a group can be quite distressing. Therefore the activities that follow emphasize the importance of functioning well in a group, ensuring that *all* individual strengths are recognized.

ACTIVITY

Everyone Wins

Target age: 6 to 10
Goal: To help children experience joy in cooperating with others to reach a desired goal
Materials needed: Balloons
Script: This game can be played with one child, but works much better if there are several players.

As with most games, the object here is to win. You will win by reaching 50 points—one point is earned each time you tap one of the balloons in the air before it hits the ground. The rules are simple:

- When your group reaches a total score of 50, everyone wins.
- Everyone gets to play.
- Everyone must work together.

I will count from 1 to 50, and when I say begin, one of you hits the balloon up in the air, and everyone tries to keep hitting it so that it does not touch the ground. One point for each hit, no matter who does it. If you miss the balloon, or if the balloon falls to the floor, then everyone "freezes," and we will start again.

What do you think is the point of this game? How does the game help you all to work better as a group? Which is more fun, cooperating with your team mates, or competing with them? Why do you think so?

Adaptation for older children: If this seems too simple for older children, try changing the pace of the game. You can do this by counting the number of seconds between hits. For a fast game, the balloon must be hit within a maximum of, say, two seconds. For a slower game, *it must not be hit* for a minimum of three seconds. Sometimes a really slow or really fast pace makes the hitting of balloons more fun!

ACTIVITY

 8G

Toothpick Masterpiece

Target age: 6 to 15

Goal: To help children work together to create and complete a collaborative project, which requires listening to and acknowledging others' ideas. This strategy calls for at least two children

Materials needed: Small boxes of toothpicks; glue stick (one of each per pair of children)

Script: You're going to work with a partner for this activity, and you've got a box of toothpicks you can use in your group of two to create something interesting. Anything and everything is acceptable—you might make a design, or a sculpture, or you might create something that's more realistic or more abstract. [Explain to younger children what these terms mean.] The rules are that each partner gets a chance to participate in the creation, and each partner helps to decide what that creation will be.

Give the players 10 to 15 minutes to work with the toothpicks. When they are finished, invite them to examine the creations that others came up with, and to share their ideas and processes with other children in the room. Some questions for discussion are:

- How did you decide to create your final product?
- Did you have any problems coming up with an idea for your creation?
- Did you have any problems working together to make it?
- How did you negotiate about how to work together?
- What would you do differently next time?

ACTIVITY

Amalgam Man

Target age: 6 to 15
Goal: To help your child work with others; to create an image that provides a joint sense of pride
Materials needed: Large piece of drawing paper (16″ × 20″ or larger); crayons, markers, colored pencils
Script: This activity works really well with children in groups of four. If you have fewer children, that's absolutely fine, and you can fill in as a member of the group to provide an additional perspective.

You're going to work together today to draw a person who doesn't exist. This person only lives in your own imaginations. This person is going to come into existence because of you—all of the members of this group. As you create the drawing of this person, you'll use *each other's best features* as inspiration for the drawing. For example, you might admire Talia's hair or eyes, and use them in your drawing. You might like Matthew's sense of humor, so you can draw a big smile to represent that on your imaginary person. Different characteristics of different people can be incorporated into the drawing in many ways.

If you notice children struggling or feeling shy about sharing their ideas, you might offer suggestions to them that can help their ideas begin to flow, such as "What would you say is Bobby's most attractive feature?" The drawing itself is secondary to the close examination of each other's admirable qualities.

As your child increases his repertoire of strategies to interact with others, he will gain valuable skills that transfer to other relationships. It is to the subject of relationships that we turn in the chapter that follows.

Part IV

Relationship Skills

9

Building Successful Friendships

Piglet sidled up to Pooh from behind. "Pooh?" he whispered.
"Yes, Piglet?"
"Nothing," said Piglet, taking Pooh's hand. "I just wanted to be sure
of you."[1]

There is something deeply elementary about the desire to be connected to others, and to feel that others wish to connect with us.[2] This mutually reciprocal linking is known by different names, but for our purposes, we will focus on friendships. The friendship between Winnie-the-Pooh and Piglet resonates with readers of all ages, contributing to the seemingly timeless appeal of A.A. Milne's stories and characters. Piglet's need to feel "sure" of Winnie reflects this deeply rooted human need.

The need to be connected contributes to the rise in social media usage among children and teens, and in the age of the "selfie" it's practically radical to think about children thinking about others as much as themselves. However, research indicates that when we think about other people our minds actually expand.[3] There are portions of our brain that respond when we think kind, compassionate thoughts, and over time—as with any exercise—we can strengthen these parts of our brain and contribute to a happier, healthier society at the same time. The following activities encourage

[1] Milne, 1992, p. 120.
[2] Maslow, 1998.
[3] Weng et al., 2013.

Your Child's Social and Emotional Well-Being: A Complete Guide for Parents and Those Who Help Them, First Edition. John S. Dacey, Lisa B. Fiore, and Steven Brion-Meisels.
© 2016 John Wiley & Sons, Ltd. Published 2016 by John Wiley & Sons, Ltd.
Companion website: www.wiley.com/go/daceywellbeing

your child to expand her own mind with respect to compassion, to tolerate and appreciate the uniqueness of others, and to develop a greater repertoire of connections. Compassionate people are good at making friends.

Activities that Foster Compassion

Compassion is a marvel of human nature, a precious inner resource, and the foundation of our well-being and the harmony of our societies. If, therefore, we seek happiness for ourselves, we should practice compassion; and if we seek happiness for others, we should also practice compassion![4]

When His Holiness the Dalai Lama speaks of empathy, his very being underscores the message. He literally lives, breathes, and practices acts of compassion every day. For most people, this art takes time and discipline.

In a famous study, in which participants were observed acting compassionately or not when confronted with a person in need of help, researchers found that "whether a person helps or not is an instant decision likely to be situationally controlled. How a person helps involves a more complex and considered number of decisions, including the time and scope to permit personality characteristics to shape them."[5] The factor that had the greatest influence on people's decisions whether or not to help the "victim" in this study was time. The researchers established different time conditions, "high-hurry" and "low-hurry." The hypothesis was that people who encounter possible helping conditions while in a hurry will be less likely to offer help than people who aren't in a hurry. This hypothesis was supported by the research. Often, when people reflect on their own capacity to behave in a compassionate, ethical manner, they face dilemmas of conscience.

Psychologist and author Howard Gardner writes, "Ethical and professional dilemmas are not new. And many would argue, with some justification, that the ways to deal with them have long been known." And yet "Much evil has been carried out in the name of religion, and many once-idolized figures … turn out to have had notable character flaws."[6] The role that empathy plays in prompting acts of compassion cannot be discounted. The role of others' concern and affection is crucial to our species' survival and well-being.[7]

[4]   Dalai Lama & Norman, 2011.
[5]   Darley & Batson, 1973.
[6]   Gardner, Csikszentmihalyi, & Damon, 2001, pp. 4–5.
[7]   Dalai Lama & Norman, 2011.

Empathy is rarely taught explicitly at home or at school, perhaps because it's often "considered intuitive and therefore difficult to teach, or a 'soft' emotional skill."[8]

Evidence does indeed support the idea that humans are born possessing an inclination toward helping others. Infants have shown a clear preference for "helpers" over "hinderers" before they are able to speak. This indicates that "humans engage in social evaluation far earlier in development than previously thought, and supports the view that the capacity to evaluate individuals on the basis of their social interactions is universal and unlearned."[9] The following activities tap into your child's capacity for compassion, sharpening the qualities that will make them easier to access and summon as needed. These activities give your child opportunities to notice what people need, and how she might help them meet those needs.

ACTIVITY

9A

Noticing Tray

Target age: 10 to 15

Goal: To encourage your child to pay attention to and remember specific items

Materials needed: A cookie sheet or tray; 10–15 miscellaneous items that are familiar to your child, such as food, toys, utensils, tools

Script: Using a cookie sheet or other serving tray, place about a dozen different items on it and place the tray in open view while your child is engaged in another activity, such as eating dinner or breakfast. At some point during the meal (or other activity), give your child a piece of paper and ask her to write the numbers 1 through 12 (or however many items are on the tray) on the paper. Then remove the tray and ask your child to write down how many items she is able to recall. Allow her to take as much time as she needs to

---

[8]   Galinksy, 2010, p. 71.

[9]   Hamlin, Wynn, & Bloom, 2007.

come up with her answers. Next, show her the tray and see how many items she was able to remember. As you discuss this, explain to her:

Just because something is in plain sight doesn't mean that you actually notice it. Are there other situations you can think of where a similar thing occurred, such as during a school assignment? How about during an outing with friends? What else do you remember about a time when you either missed something obvious or paid attention to something that wasn't as important as something else?

Adaptation for younger children: Put the cookie sheet or tray on a table and give your child a few minutes to look carefully at the items. Then tell her to close her eyes, and while she's not looking remove one or two items. Once you have removed the item(s), ask her to look at the tray again and notice which item(s) are missing. This may be repeated a few times, with different items being removed each time. Then you may wish to hide the entire tray, and see how many items she can recall from memory. Talk with your child about how it sometimes takes real effort and focus to notice something, and how this is very true of noticing people's needs.

ACTIVITY

I Spy What You Need

Target age: 11 to 15
Goal: To encourage your child to notice the needs of others
Materials needed: No materials needed if you are able to find a bench in a park, on a sidewalk, or in a mall, where you and your child can sit and watch people as they go about their activities. If you aren't able to sit in this way, then two or three illustrated children's books or magazines with rich illustrations (or two or three film/video clips that show many people and/or city scenes) can be substituted for the first-hand experience of observing people in action.

Script: We are going to play a game where we try to notice the needs of others. We're going to sit here for a few minutes and see what we see. What do you notice about the people around us? Can you see something that could help them, or would be nice to do for them?

For every need that your child is able to identify, give her one point. For every possible action that she might take to help the individuals meet those perceived needs, give your child two points. You may use the same point system for yourself or other children who might be participating with your child.

The object isn't to be competitive, but instead to keep score and use the score as a reference for future playing. This is a somewhat strange scoring system, because if everyone had their individual needs met, then there wouldn't be any points to be had! There would be no unmet needs. Since this isn't the current reality for most people, and most of them do not have the good fortune to have every single need met in an immediate fashion, there should be ample opportunity for your child to identify needs of others. You can vary locations to see how different locations lend themselves to different levels of awareness. Other variations include different times of year, different kinds of weather, and so on.

Adaptation for younger children: Younger children can participate in this activity without the points component, although some children will find the motivation of accruing points fun. You can model for your child what you notice about others, and how you would help, if possible.

ACTIVITY

Dining Needs Challenge

Target age: 6 to 10

Goal: To encourage your child to notice the needs of others and to attempt to help others meet their respective needs

Materials needed: Mealtime items, such as plates, silverware, cups, food, and/or condiments, spices

Script: Set the table as you would for any family meal, leaving out certain items. For example, you might place plates at everyone's seat except for one person's seat. You might give everyone a napkin except one or two people. Perhaps you serve soup and all but one person has a spoon at her seat. For that matter, the salt or pepper shaker could be missing, or the favorite bottle of hot sauce isn't on the table for taco night. The missing items should be left where they're typically kept. Once everyone is seated, simply ask:

Does everyone have everything they need? Your goal is to notice the needs of others and try to help people meet their needs by identifying and retrieving the missing items. Please let me see you do that. Why was that a good thing to do?

Adaptations for older children: Older children can take charge of the activity by setting the table and choosing which items are missing. As they get used to this exercise, they can come up with new variations of the activity, such as bringing items to a picnic, to the beach, to a baseball game, and so on.

It can be helpful to have a brief discussion with your child about the difference between *needing* something and *wanting* something. In the children's novel *Justin Case: Shells, Smells, and the Horrible Flip-flops of Doom*, the title character—fourth-grader, Justin—has the following exchange with his first-grade sister:

> I sank down into my chair and rested my damp face in my hands, listening to the bus pull away from my house without me. "I need a plan," I said.
> "No, Justin," Elizabeth said, patting my arm. "All you need is food, water, shelter, and especially an umbrella. Everything else is a want."[10]

At different ages and in different moods, children are more or less able to identify the needs of others. Often, there are values and judgments inherent

---

[10]   Vail, 2012.

in these awarenesses. Someone who looks like she needs a new pair of shoes might be assumed to be poor or out of work. Other judgments can range from the mild to the extreme, and include assumptions and biases. The activities that follow encourage your child to develop an mindfulness of differences, as well as an appreciation for them.

Activities that Foster Tolerance and Appreciation

"When you wake up in the morning, Pooh," said Piglet at last, "what's the first thing you say to yourself?"
"What's for breakfast?" said Pooh. "What do you say, Piglet?"
"I say, I wonder what's going to happen exciting today?" said Piglet.
"It's the same thing," he said.[11]

As Piglet and Winnie demonstrate, close friends can often find common ground without actually sharing the same opinion, whether it is your child's favorite flavor of ice cream, the same music, or the same preference in weekend pastimes. Although it is sometimes these simple things that initially attract us to friends, the deepest of friendships are those that are built on strong foundations. These foundations support and celebrate the differences that make each of us unique.

ACTIVITY

9D

Fill My Cup, Fill Me Up

Target age: 6 to 10
Goal: To teach your child the power that underlies giving someone a genuine compliment or acts of encouragement
Materials needed: Index cards or other pieces of paper; pens/pencils; a teacup or other cup

---

[11]   Milne, 2005, p. 160.

Script: Your child may be familiar with the "fill a bucket" books by Carol McCloud.[12] Many school communities have used these books as launch pads for school-wide efforts to be kind to others. These books also help to establish shared vocabulary or language to use when discussing feelings. Another way of framing this is to think about a simple cup. When someone does something nice for you, or makes you feel happy, you can say,

You filled my cup! Have you ever heard of the term "put-down"? Can you give some examples of put-downs you've heard from others: friends, grown-ups, or in movies or TV programs? What might the opposite of a put-down be called, and how might it help fill someone's cup?" Your child may say a "put-up," or "build-up." Whatever you think sounds positive and supportive is terrific. Can you think of some examples of that could fill your own cup, such as, "I like how you know when I'm nervous and distract me so I think of something else," or "You always make me feel special when I'm feeling blue."

Designate a specific time during the day or evening when the family members fill each other's cups. This could be during a mealtime, at bedtime, or any other time that is easy to turn into a routine. You can keep a pad of post-it notes or other paper in a designated area next to family members' cups, so that anyone who wishes to fill someone's cup is able to do so. As you begin doing this with your child, you'll start to notice different strengths and inclinations that you and other family members have. You can discuss with your child how everyone brings different personality traits and skills to the family, and to different situations.

Adaptation for older children: Older children benefit from this activity in many ways, particularly when they feel concerned about how they compare to classmates. It is helpful to keep praise anchored in their genuine efforts, as opposed to labels such as "smart" or "pretty" or "strong." Such adjectives, although momentarily pleasing, often come with expectations that they must be maintained.

---

[12] McCloud & Martin, 2008; McCloud, 2006.

ACTIVITY

Snowflake Cake

Target age: 6 to 10

Goal: To encourage your child to think about uniqueness

Materials needed: White pieces of paper, cut into squares approximately 5″ × 5″ wide; scissors; glue; a large piece of construction paper with the outline of a round "cake" drawn on it, or wall/window surface with round "cake" image drawn with erasable or glass-safe markers

Script: Snowflakes are both alike and different. Scientists tell us that no two snowflakes are alike, yet they are made of the same molecules. They share the same air space, yet they float on their own paths as they swirl, drift, collide, and eventually land. People are a lot like snowflakes. We might be similar in many ways, yet we are not the same. What are some ways that people are alike?

Your child should list some ways that people are alike, such as, "We all have skin and hair and eyes and noses," or "We all are scared sometimes," or "No one is ever perfect." Then ask your child to think about and share some ways that people are different. She might describe different tastes in food, different physical attributes, or different languages and traditions that people have. Explain to your child that just as the world is home to billions of different people, she can create a "Snowflake Cake" that represents the different "ingredients" or qualities that she—or your family—possesses. Taking one piece of white paper at a time, your child can cut out snowflake shapes. This is accomplished by taking the square piece of paper and folding it in half, and then again into fourths. Your child can experiment with different folding techniques and the number of times she folds the paper. Often, the thickness of the paper and your child's ability to cut through the folded paper dictate how many folds she will make. As your child cuts each paper snowflake, ask her one quality of her own that she can write on each snowflake. She might, for example, write "blue eyes," "shares with others," and "silly" on her snowflakes. Each of the snowflakes can be taped or glued to the cake, so that eventually the surface of the paper, wall, or window will be full of snowflakes. Your child can decide in advance whether she wants to create her own cake or a family cake. If she chooses to create a family cake, she might want to invite other family members to contribute, and she can see how they all work together to create a final product.

Adaptation for older children: Older children can extend this activity by creating a collage on a computer, for example. Different online tools, such as Ribbet! and iPiccy, offer engaging options for children and adults.

While each of us is unique, we also function daily as part of a larger group. This group can be as local as the family unit or a class at school, or as far-reaching as the country we live in. The activities that follow demonstrate to your child how she can build upon elements such as compassion and kindness as well as respect for individual strengths and challenges. As we embark on our own unique journeys, it is always comforting to realize that we are part of a larger community that can, figuratively and literally, nurture and sustain us.

Activities that Foster Connectedness

*So he took hold of Pooh's front paws and Rabbit took hold of
Christopher Robin, and all Rabbit's friends and relations took hold of
Rabbit, and they all pulled together...
And for a long time Pooh only said "Ow!"...
And "Oh!"...
And then all of a sudden, he said "Pop!" just as if a cork were coming
out of a bottle.
And Christopher Robin and Rabbit and all Rabbit's friends and
relations went head-over-heels backwards ... and on top of them came
Winnie-the-Pooh—free!
So, with a nod of thanks to his friends, he went on with his walk
through the forest, humming proudly to himself. But, Christopher
Robin looked after him lovingly, and said to himself, "Silly old Bear!"*[13]

[13] Milne, 2005, pp. 32–33.

This final quote in this chapter from *Winnie-the-Pooh* illustrates the point made at the end of the previous activity: often it is our connection to others that sustains us. The phrase "it takes a village" was coined in 1996 by then First Lady Hillary Rodham Clinton. The sentiment underlying that phrase was that it takes many people working together to ensure the health and success of America's children. The phrase has been adopted and adapted to fit other situations, and the common criterion is that it requires more than one individual—a village—to ensure the desired outcome. In his book *Finding Your Element*, Sir Ken Robinson describes a tribe as:

> a group of people who share the same interests and passions. The tribe may be large or small. It can exist virtually, through social media or in person. Tribes may be highly diverse. They may cross generations and cultures. They may cross time and include people who are no longer living but whose lives and legacy continue to inspire those who are. You may be a member of various tribes at the same time or at different points in your life. What defines tribes are their shared passions. Connecting with people who share your Element can have tremendous benefits for you and for them. They include affirmation, collaboration and inspiration.[14]

The experience of connecting with others who share similar passions contributes to the child's growing sense of self and belonging. Many of the social and emotional skills articulated in this book will make connections with others easier for your child. For example, a child who is able to adapt well to change, who is self aware, and who is empathetic will more naturally relate well to others. The same may be said of a child who is able to maintain a healthy balance in her life (i.e., between work and play), and who appreciates the idea that every day brings something for which she can feel gratitude.

The following activities promote a greater awareness of ways to establish new connections, and to reflect on existing connections with others.

[14] Robinson & Aronica, 2013.

ACTIVITY

Connection Kits

Target age: 6 to 10

Goal: To teach your child about the many different qualities inherent in connections with others

Materials needed: Plastic sandwich bags, preferably Ziploc or another variety that closes/zips; assorted items for the bags, such as one each of buttons, small rocks, adhesive bandages, cotton balls, stickers, rubber bands, paper clips, and pennies

Script: Discuss with your child what she thinks each item in the bag might represent for her, with respect to friendships. For example, a paper clip could represent how *friends stay together*, a button could remind your child that *friends help us feel secure*. Similarly, an adhesive bandage might prompt her to think that *friends can heal what hurts us*, a rubber band can remind us that *friends sometimes stretch us*, and a penny could indicate that *friends are priceless*. There are many variations that your child may think up, and these ideas can open pathways to larger, meaningful conversations.

Adaptation for older children: Older children can use these ideas in the concrete, tangible form described above, or can choose to write short poems about friends using these analogies. Haikus present an ideal format for concise language—the traditional format is a three-line poem, with the lines containing syllables in a 5-7-5 sequence. An example of this is:

> *Like sticky pink gum*
> *Susan will stay by my side*
> *Someone I can trust*

ACTIVITY

 9G

Likeable Links

Target age: 6 to 10

Goal: To help your child recognize the many qualities of friendship that exist and how to strengthen bonds between people

Materials needed: Colorful strips of paper; stapler or tape; markers, crayons, or other writing tools

Script: Present your child with the strips of construction paper, or work together to cut the paper into strips. Invite your child to decorate the strips with words and/or images that she considers essential to being a good friend.

Who are some people that you call your friends? What are some specific qualities that these friends possess that make you happy to know them? How do they make you feel good about yourself? How do they challenge your thinking or help you to reach for new goals?

As your child decorates the strips of paper, connect the links to form a chain. Your child should feel free to add links as she thinks of new qualities or people. Display the chain in the house or in her room. Encourage her to continue adding strips to the friendship chain over time. Discuss what happens when the chain breaks—how can it be repaired? How does this really happen with people, as opposed to just on paper?

Adaptation for older children: Older children can examine examples of friendship from literature, television, and film to extend their ideas about connections between people. Some seem likely and others seem unusual yet seem to last, so include: Felix Unger and Oscar Madison from *The Odd Couple*, Hermione Granger and Ron Weasley from the *Harry Potter* series, Tina Fey and Amy Poehler (on- and off-screen).

ACTIVITY

Companion Collage

Target age: 6 to 10

Goal: To help your child recognize that many different feelings and attributes contribute to who we are

Materials needed: Magazines; scissors; glue; a large piece of construction paper (at least 8½" × 11") or a paper shopping bag that has been cut into a large rectangle, with the outline of a person's body drawn on it. Note: this outline will be filled in with the pieces of magazines that your child chooses to cut out and glue onto the paper, representing many qualities of friendship and companionship.

Script: Present your child with the large piece of paper and say,

What do you notice about this shape of a person? It's rather empty, isn't it? What are some feelings that someone might feel if she felt as empty as this outline?

Answers may represent a range of feelings, including sad, lonely, peaceful, quiet, bored, or other.

What fills someone up? How does friendship or connection to others make a person feel more complete or whole?

Invite your child to look at pictures in the various magazines that you have provided.

Find some pictures that remind you of what's important in a friend or companion. You can choose pictures that remind you of your own friendships or your own interests, or choose images that you find exciting!

She should feel free to choose and cut out any images that resonate with her about some feature or quality of connection. When the images have been selected, your child can glue them to the paper to create a collage. Display the collage someplace in the home where it is highly visible. From time to time, you might ask your child about features on the paper, and if she would update any parts of the collage.

Adaptation for older children: Older children may enjoy using other materials to represent their ideas, such as sculpture with clay, recyclables, or wood, sewing or other fabric/textile creations, or using digital technology online to create a collage (see Activity 9E above).

The activity above presents an opportunity to make visible what we often cannot readily see—what one person values in another, yearns for in a relationship, or holds sacred in personal connection.

> To be able to see the other person's story from the inside you'll need some specific skills in inquiring, listening, and acknowledgment. To share your own story with clarity and power, you need to feel entitled and be precise in speaking only for yourself.[15]

As some experts suggest, "Only after you begin to change a relationship can you really see it."[16]

Parents and caregivers play a vital role in helping children "see" and understand the dynamics that exist in friendships. The chapter that follows provides examples of how important social and emotional learning skills are the hallmark of strong leaders.

[15] Stone, Patton, & Heen, 1999, p. 162.
[16] Lerner, 1985, p. 195.

10

Demonstrating Leadership

It is better to lead from behind and to put others in front, especially when you celebrate victory when nice things occur. You take the front line when there is danger. Then people will appreciate your leadership.

Nelson Mandela

Effective leaders:

- Want their people to succeed.
- Are not competitive with their team.
- Have an open-door policy (generous with their time).
- Would rather err on the side of grace than be just or strict with policies.
- Are open to new ideas.
- Freely share what they are learning.
- Love to give credit to others even when they could rightly keep it for themselves.
- Care about their team. They know about each team member's goals and dreams, and diligently try to help them fulfill those desires.[1]

[1] Stevens, 2015, p. 1.

Your Child's Social and Emotional Well-Being: A Complete Guide for Parents and Those Who Help Them, First Edition. John S. Dacey, Lisa B. Fiore, and Steven Brion-Meisels.
© 2016 John Wiley & Sons, Ltd. Published 2016 by John Wiley & Sons, Ltd.
Companion website: www.wiley.com/go/daceywellbeing

The statements that open this chapter highlight qualities that distinguish a successful leader—competence and self-awareness. These qualities are two of the traits that the Collaborative for Academic, Social and Emotional Learning (CASEL, the leader of SEL in the United States; see Chapters 1 and 7) identifies as central to an individual's success in life. CASEL also holds that there are qualities that establish someone as a leader (e.g., distinguishing responsibility from obligation; responsibility to self and others; staying in touch with what matters most).[2]

Congressman Tim Ryan says, "America has always been defined by how we have responded to crisis."[3] Ryan notes that mindful practices are essential to his own work as a leader in his congressional district, and how they have inspired him and others in the pursuit of success. For children and adults alike, ordinary pursuits may feel similar to managing a crisis because of one's level of stress or lack of self-confidence. A colleague once said that people are so busy "starring in their own operas" that they aren't aware of the deficiencies in themselves that they bemoan in others.

Author and meditation teacher Sharon Salzberg has identified several skills that she contends are critical for happiness—the optimal desired outcome of social/emotional leadership. She posits that success in the workplace is most likely when eight pillars are in place. These pillars are also important for children:

- *Balance.* The ability to differentiate between who you are and what your job is.
- *Concentration.* The ability to focus without being swayed by distractions.
- *Compassion.* Being aware of and sympathetic to the humanity of others.
- *Resilience.* The ability to recover from defeat, frustration, or failure.
- *Communication and connection.* Understanding that everything we do and say can improve connection or weaken it.
- *Integrity.* Integrating your deepest ethical values into all you do.
- *Meaning.* Infusing the work you do with relevance for your own personal goals.
- *Open awareness.* The ability to see the big picture and not be held back by self-imposed limitations.[4]

[2] CASEL, 2014.
[3] Ryan, 2012, p. 1.
[4] Salzberg, 2013, p. 5.

For children in school, their daily lives involve "work," and their "jobs" entail these precise skills. As we grow throughout our lifetimes, the setting may change, but the fundamental skills that help us succeed remain constant.

The ability to bring attention to these details is a primary task of leadership.[5] This includes paying attention to more than one's personal needs. Authentic leadership requires the "bandwidth" and flexibility to help guide a group or organization. One element that has been acknowledged recently in the media is "focus." Psychologist Daniel Goleman states: "Leadership itself hinges on effectively capturing and directing the collective attention. Leading attention requires these elements: first, focusing your own attention, then attracting and directing attention from others, and getting and keeping the attention of employees and peers, of customers and clients."[6]

For example, a focused leader is able to influence a group's leanings. Negative thoughts and feelings may be addressed directly. Complex problems that exist in an organization, whether it is a family, a classroom, or a workplace, are most successfully resolved through collaborative effort, guided by thoughtful, engaged leadership.

Such leadership need not be grand or glamorous. In *When Fish Fly*, author John Yokoyama shares his recognizing in himself the ability to lead others: "You can come to work and affect the world for the better. You can matter in the lives of others. You can share a powerful vision with your team and create breakthrough success, and, yes, you can do all that while throwing and selling fish."[7]

Popular media and characters from literature dating back to the Old Testament portray leaders as being in positions of power. The situations that these traditional examples of leaders find themselves in often include conflict, such as battles and struggles for control over people and possessions. Providing insight into power, Congressman Tim Ryan notes that our perceptions have been influenced over thousands of years by "millennia of warrior traditions … focused on training two qualities: wisdom and bravery. Wisdom is defined as the ability to see clearly how things are, not how we want them to be, and then use that information to make the most effective decision in the moment. Bravery … is the ability to stay present with any experience, even an extremely difficult one, without needing it to be different."[8]

[5]   Goleman, Boyatzis, & McKee, 2013, p. 209.
[6]   Goleman et al., 2013, p. 210.
[7]   Yokoyama, 2004, p. 24.
[8]   Ryan, 2012, p. 116.

The Army Leadership Challenge

In most countries throughout the world, the people being trained as officers face a similar test: how good are they at leadership? As an important part of their evaluation, each trainee is called upon to lead a group of five enlisted persons across a guarded road. If any of the soldiers is spotted attempting to cross, the activity is stopped and the officer trainee has failed the test.

What the leader doesn't know is that each of the soldiers has been prepped to be uncooperative. For example, the first soldier to attempt the crossing falls down halfway, and barely escapes detection. Another makes it part way across, then comes back asking for directions about what to do on the other side. Finally, the fifth soldier feigns terror at being discovered, and refuses to attempt the crossing.

If the leader becomes angry at the team's lack of cooperation, or fails to imagine alternative instructions to achieve the task, she or he is considered to be a poor candidate for rapid advancement up the ranks.

What do you think of this test of leadership? The following activities will help your child come to understand power as connected to self and others, and to recognize that the power to think out a situation is as important as the power to have control over others.

Activities that Promote Understanding of Power

ACTIVITY

Whatever Lies within Our Power to Do...

Target age: 11 to 15
Goal: To help your child recognize qualities that he associates with power

Materials needed: Paper and pencils/pens for writing, or your own electronic device

Script: Let's think about power. When you hear the word "power," who comes into your mind? On your paper, write down the names of between five and 10 of the most powerful people you know or know about. These can be people you have met or people you have seen or heard about on television or online.

When your child has completed his list, use the questions below as a basis for conversation:

- Are all of these people really leaders? If so, how do you know, and whom do they lead?
- How do you know these people are powerful?
- How do they use their power?
- Do you believe that these people think they are powerful?
- What do these people have in common?
- How are these individuals different?

Adaptations for younger children: Show your child pictures of people who represent power. These can be from magazines, cartoons, or favorite stories. Ask him how he knows that someone is powerful. His answers will likely vary when he's speaking about fictional or real people, and this will give you an opportunity to talk about the differences between human and imaginary traits.

ACTIVITY

 10B

Who's the Boss?

Target age: 11 to 15

Goal: To give your child the opportunity to influence decision-making

Materials needed: Paper and pencils; sheet of paper with suggested tasks written on it (see below)

Script: Have your child get together with some of his friends for this activity.

Now is your chance to be the "boss" for a while. While you are the boss, you are allowed to give anyone here any of the instructions on this sheet:

Suggested Tasks Sheet

- Quack like a duck.
- Sing "Happy Birthday."
- Walk in a circle three times.
- Hop on one foot and clap your hands for 20 seconds.
- Walk up to someone and ask him what time it is.
- Press your thumbs against your earlobes and waggle your fingers.

Once your child has given people the instructions on the list, the following questions can be used as launching points for conversation:

- What did you like about being the boss? How did it feel?
- How did it feel to be told what to do?
- How would you feel if you were the boss all the time?
- How would you feel if you were never the leader?
- How can someone be a better boss?
- What power do people usually have over you?
- What power do you usually have over other people?
- What power do you have over yourself?

Adaptations for younger children: Younger children will have no trouble talking about people who enforce rules and therefore exert power over their lives. Your child can be the boss, the teacher, the king, or any other figure that he deems powerful.

As children develop skills and strategies tied to decision-making—big and small—they learn to make choices about what to ignore and where to focus their attention. This awareness brings with it a responsibility to balance difficult, sometimes contrary elements in order to achieve a desired outcome. Congressman Ryan refers to this as "the ability to be firm and simultaneously to be gentle. This can be challenging, but Martin Luther King, Jr. offered us an example of holding hard and soft together. He pointed out that love without power is ineffectual, and power without love is destructive."[9]

ACTIVITY

King/Queen of the "Have To's"

Target age: 6 to 10

Goal: To help your child understand the difference between wanting and needing to do something, and having the power to choose

Materials needed: Paper and pencil

Script: We're going to talk about the difference between things that we have to do, and things that we want to do. Let's start by writing down five things that you have to do at home or at school. You can use the following sentence starter, "I have to _____" and complete this statement four more times. When you're finished, rewrite the sentences using the following sentence starter, "I want to _____."

The following questions can be used to start conversation about the activity:

- Which of the "I want to..." sentences also should be included as "I have to..." things?
- Who decides whether or not you "have to" do something?
- What is the difference between something that you have to do because you believe you must and something that you have to do because someone else tells you to do it?
- How do you decide whether or not you "have to" do something?
- What happens if you choose not to do something you "have to" do?

Adaptations for older children: Older children can benefit from this activity as it is written, but you can enhance the conversation by

---

[9] Ryan, 2012, p. 169.

introducing situations in current society or fictional stories that your child may be reading in school. For example, you can request his thinking about the best ways to deal with climate change (storminess of the weather in recent years) or global health issues (the Ebola crisis).

ACTIVITY

The END??? Actions and Consequences

Target age: 11 to 15

Goal: To help your child recognize that his choices have consequences

Materials needed: Examples from comic books or *Choose Your Own Adventure* novels, where the endings are ambiguous, cliff-hangers, or otherwise undetermined

Script: Have you ever noticed that when you make a decision, sometimes things work out fine and sometimes there are surprises? No matter how hard we might try to think of all of the risks involved in making a decision, we may forget a detail or two.

It's helpful to recognize that there can often be several successful endings or outcomes connected with one specific decision. Let's look at a situation in this comic book/novel. Try to find a scene where the character(s) made an important decision. How might the character(s) have handled the situation differently? If you were to write an alternate ending, what would it be?

Take a few moments to write or sketch out a story that relates to the one in the comic book/novel. Make it relate to yourself if you can. Let's talk about the many decisions you could choose from, and what factors you might consider.

Adaptations for younger children: Young children can follow this activity in much the same way as older children, substituting a favorite children's book for the comic book or novel.

Leadership entails skill in handling and distributing power, and making calculated choices. Also implicit in the notion of leadership is the understanding that others choose to follow the inspiration of a leader.

> Leaders who inspire can articulate shared values that resonate with and motivate the group. These are the leaders people love to work with, who surface the vision that moves everyone. But to speak from the heart, to the heart, a leader must first know her values. That takes self-awareness.[10]

Self-awareness, a vital aspect of leadership, includes having an accurate image of one's strengths and weaknesses. This affords children the opportunity to view themselves as protagonists, directors, and authors of their own stories.

Activities that Promote Self-awareness

> It seems to me it would do us all good to act from our heart more often. We'll be surprised how small acts of attention and kindness can release the energy, enthusiasm, and imagination bottled up in our overstressed minds and bodies. We have tried a million times to think our way to a better society. But our thinking doesn't work so well if it's not aligned with what we feel deep in our hearts, our inspirations and aspirations, our innermost desire. We need to re-align ourselves the way a GPS in a car recalibrates the route. When our wandering mind takes us away from our heart, we need to pause and realign ourselves with the values we have stored there.[11]

Leaders who have a strong awareness of themselves are better able to gain the trust of others. Former president of Wellesley College Diana Walsh stated in a lecture, "Trustworthy leadership begins and ends with leaders who can question themselves."[12] The following activities are designed to expand children's capacity to examine their own motives.

[10]   Goleman et al., 2013, p. 225.
[11]   Ryan, 2012, p. 31.
[12]   Walsh, 2013.

ACTIVITY

  10E

Personal Shield/Family Crest

1. Most happy event in your life

2. Your greatest achievement

3. You are good at

4. Would like to do someday

5. You'd like to become better at

Personal Shield: _____

Target age: 6 to 10

Goal: To help children recognize their own strengths and connection to others

Materials needed: Papers with shield/crest printed on them (see model above—leave the five sections empty so your child can draw her own pictures in them); crayons, markers, colored pencils. Note: this activity works well with several children.

Script: We are going to celebrate what makes you special and what makes you feel proud to be yourself. Look at your shield and use the drawing materials to color in the different parts of the shield, matching the number on the part of the shield to the following questions:

1. Draw a picture here of the most happy event in your life.
2. Draw a picture here of your (or your family's) greatest achievement.
3. Draw a picture here of something you are good at.
4. Draw a picture here of something you would like to do or be someday.
5. Draw a picture of something you'd like to become better at.

Give the children 15 minutes to work on their shields.

When you've finished, share your shield with someone. When you have listened to someone share his shield and the images he's drawn, take a moment to share back with him something that you have learned about him today. If you have a few questions that you would like to ask, feel free to ask and learn more about each other.

Adaptations for older children: Older children will enjoy this activity as written, and can also create 3-D shields using art materials or recyclables in your home (perhaps on large sheet of oak tag). They should feel free to use items that represent their ideas as well as writing brief explanations on the front or back of the shield.

ACTIVITY

My Symbols of Success

Target age: 6 to 10

Goal: To help your child remember past and/or current successes or accomplishments and to note the effort it took to make these happen

Materials needed: Objects that represent success or accomplishment. This activity works well with several children

Script: Before you do this activity with your child, ask him to name three objects that remind him of past success, objects that make him feel proud. Examples might be a Boy Scout badge, a sports award, or a report card.

You've named three objects that make you feel proud—let's look at the objects you chose to share. People tend to save objects because they can mean so much—the objects remind us of our own abilities, relationships with others, fun places we've been, or adventures that we've had. These objects then become symbols—a symbol represents something else, often something that happened to you. Many people save pictures, poems, trophies, stories from newspapers or magazines, ticket stubs, and other items. Pick one of the objects that you named and tell me (or partners if in a small group) about what you've chosen. You may want to share some of the feelings or meanings that the object brings up for you.

- Does this object represent a goal that you set for yourself?
- Was the accomplishment a happy accident?
- What are some goals that you wish to achieve for yourself in the next year? In the next ten years? In your lifetime?

Adaptation for older children: You can ask older children to name eight objects, or actually go and get those objects. You can also expect a deeper consideration of the relevance of the items.

ACTIVITY

 10G

Through the Goalpost!

Target age: 11 to 15

Goal: To help your child set reasonable goals and mark progress toward achieving them

Materials needed: Bulletin board; construction paper or other paper that can be used to decorate the bulletin board; 3″ × 5″ index cards or other small pieces of paper (cut in the shape of footballs, if you have the time and/or inclination); pencils or pens for writing goals on the paper.

Script: In advance of this activity, decorate the bulletin board to resemble a football goalpost, or enlist the help of your child in decorating it.

Let's look at this bulletin board—notice that it looks like a football goalpost. Each day you should think about a goal, or even a few goals, that you would like to achieve. Using one of these index cards, you can write down something about that goal. Take a minute or two now to write down a goal, maybe two goals, that you would like to accomplish. When you are finished you can put your card/football on the bulletin board, below the crossbar of the goalpost. Tomorrow, we can check and see how you're feeling about your goal.

When you feel that you have met the goal, you can move the card/football over the crossbar and through the goalpost. If you haven't yet met your goal, you can leave the card/football where it is and consider your progress, any obstacles you're facing, and steps needed to achieve your goal. Many goals take time to achieve, so you may need to be patient and realistic about how long it will take to get your card through that goalpost. With time and effort, I believe you will be able to meet your goals!

Adaptation for younger children: Younger children may or may not understand the football metaphor in this activity, so you can accomplish the same understanding of progress by having them move a button or penny along a ruler taped to a windowsill in a prominent place as they work toward their goal(s).

As children become more self-aware, they naturally realize that the self is part of a bigger system. They recognize that we are not alone, and that the goal is not independence from family and friends. Rather, it is interdependence with them. This often stirs questions about doing something for oneself in a selfish manner, and doing something for oneself as part of important self-care. Ultimately, children will come to understand that when we "water the seeds of peace in ourselves and those around us, we become alive, and we can help ourselves and others realize peace and compassion."[13] This is among the best goals of leadership.

ACTIVITY

Self-care Is Not Selfish

Target age: 11 to 15

Goal: To help your child understand the difference between taking care of himself and being selfish

Materials needed: Paper and pencil/pen or your own electronic device

Script: Taking care of yourself is very important. When you take care of yourself, you're then better able to lead others. There are many ways to take care of yourself, and these can be small or large—they still make a difference in how you feel, think, and act.

How do you define self-care, or legitimate care of yourself? Take a few seconds to write down any words, thoughts, or images that come to mind when you think of the phrase, "taking care of oneself." [Provide a couple of minutes for your child to write down some ideas.]

When do you think a person is being selfish? What does selfish look like? Now take a few moments to write down any words, thoughts, or images that come to mind when you hear the word "selfish." [Provide a few minutes for your child to write down some of his ideas.]

Now that you have jotted down some ideas, what are some things you can do to take care of yourself? [Examples might include exercising, eating healthy foods, getting enough sleep, asking for help, and others.] On your paper, write down some ways you can take good care of yourself so that you may be better able to reach your goals and help others.

Adaptation for younger children: Talk with your child about what he enjoys doing, and how he takes care of himself every day. He will likely

---

[13]   Nhat Hanh, 2008, p. 12.

recognize simple things like eating favorite foods, playing games with friends, and keeping warm or cool as the weather dictates. There are numerous children's books about being selfish that can be borrowed from the local library or purchased, such as *It's Mine!* by Leo Lionni and *The Berenstain Bears Get the Gimmes* by Stan and Jan Berenstain. Such books provide much to talk about.

As Goleman puts it, "[the] most visible leadership abilities build not just on empathy, but also on managing ourselves and sensing how what we do affects others."[14] Demonstrating leadership is one way that children portray their social-emotional competence. The chapters that follow build upon the distinctions and relationships between self and others.

[14] Goleman et al., 2013, p. 235.

Part V

Responsible Decision-making

11

Thinking Creatively

Probably no aspect of SEL is less measurable by multiple-choice tests, or even human evaluation, than creative thinking. And probably no aptitude is more vital to success in life. Let's take a closer look at this crucial characteristic.

First, we ask you to examine the drawing below and imagine a story about it. Let your resourcefulness flow freely, with no concern for "getting it right." Surprise yourself!

Your Child's Social and Emotional Well-Being: A Complete Guide for Parents and Those Who Help Them, First Edition. John S. Dacey, Lisa B. Fiore, and Steven Brion-Meisels.
© 2016 John Wiley & Sons, Ltd. Published 2016 by John Wiley & Sons, Ltd.
Companion website: www.wiley.com/go/daceywellbeing

Did you dream up a story you feel good about? If you think your story is creative, what makes it so? Can creativity ever be defined? Does your story help you answer these questions? If you think this strategy stimulated your imagination, here's how you might employ it with your child:

ACTIVITY

What's in the Box?

Target age: 11 to 15
Goal: To stir the creative imagination
Materials needed: The drawing of the animal in a box (above), pencil, paper, and clock (or timer)
Script: Please write a story about the scene in this box. There is no right way to write it. Be as imaginative as you can! [Allow 10 minutes.]
In one study of imaginative problem-solving by John Dacey and educational psychologist Richard Ripple,[1] 1,200 middle-school students wrote stories about this picture. Amazingly, about 900 of the stories were almost exactly alike! The other 300 stories, however, were decidedly different from each other. Were those in the last group creative? Did yours or your child's stories make the grade? The only way to judge how imaginative stories are is to compare them to stories written by numerous similar people. That is impractical, but you can get a good sense by comparing your story to these two, written by sixth-graders:

Curiosity Killed the Cat
Once upon a time there was a cat named Tom. He was very curious. One day he was looking around and spied a strange box. He heard a scratching noise coming from it. He lifted up one side and there he saw a mouse named Jerry. Jerry was a fat little mouse, and looked delishus. Not thinking, he grabbed Jerry. The box crashed down on him and broke his head. That was how curiosity killed the cat!

[1]   Dacey & Ripple, 1969.

A Tail about a Petrified Chipmunk

Joe, the chipmunk, was chasing a butterfly. He was starving.

The sky overhead was streaked with clouds. The sun when it showed barely squeezed through the trees. The burnt floor of the forest made the day seem gloomy. Joe wondered how he was going to get any food. He thought of last night—the men, the monsters. Some had four sharp claws, others had huge round eyes and pointed teeth. Joe was so scared!

Suddenly a bear jumped out of the bushes and was after him. He ran to a stream and started swimming. He was safe—only for a little, but…[The story stops here because time ran out.]

What is the major difference between these stories? The first one, of course, represents the 900 similar efforts, and the second the 300 wildly different ones. The children who wrote the ordinary stories imagined that there was a *boundary around the picture*, which restricted them. In effect, they fenced their creativity within a corral of imagined rules.

The instructions for this exercise had no rules about sticking to the two images—cat and box. In fact, the directions explicitly encouraged vivid imagining. Nevertheless, the first group of writers assumed a number of implicit limitations, and under those circumstances, it isn't surprising that there wasn't much to write about. To emphasize this point, here's a third example:

How Kuriosity Killed the Kat

This is the story about a very curious cat named Kat. One day, Kat was wandering in the woods where she came upon a big house made of fish. Without thinking she ate much of that house. The next morning when she woke up she had grown extremely larger. Even as she walked down the street she was getting bigger. Finally she got bigger than any building ever made. She walked up to the Empire State building in N. Y. C. and accidentally crushed it. The people had to think of a way to stop her, so they made this great iron box which made the cat curious. She finally got inside it but it was too heavy to get her out of again. There she lived for the rest of her life. But she was still curious until her death, which was 6,820,000 years later. They buried her in the state of Rhode Island, and I mean the whole state.

The 300 children who wrote the more imaginative stories frequently used the small square in the picture merely as a departure point from which they could travel to other, more exotic lands. Many saw it as a window or a door through which they could leave the simple scene. Others stretched their imaginations to describe it as a time capsule, a case of TNT, a casket, or a player piano. A small number disregarded the square altogether.

Adaptation for younger children: If your child is too young to write a story, ask him to dictate it to you and you write it down.

To be considered creative, must a person's achievements bring international recognition? We do not think so. As Shank and Cleary point out, simply getting through a typical day in the modern world requires imagination. "These small acts of creativity, though they differ in scope, are not different in kind from the brilliant leaps of an Einstein. Creativity is a commonplace in cognition, not an esoteric gift bequeathed only to a few."[2] So what do we know about ordinary creativity? First of all, it is not now and probably never was equally distributed throughout the world. As Zhao reports:

There were less than ten technical and social inventions between 1 AD and 1800 AD. Contrast that to the last 200 years, during which time we have seen the creation of more than 25 life-altering technological and social inventions, which had have life-altering effect on nature and quality of our lives, such as computers, antibiotics, airplanes, internet, genetic engineering, organ transplants, automobiles, lasers, telecommunication, etc. Consider this: if you had been born more than 2,000 years ago it would have been possible to live your entire life without being impacted by a life-altering invention. When you live in the 21st century, a time fraught with change, that's pretty hard to imagine. You are also aware all great societies throughout history have been great because they have done an exemplary job of meeting these two goals.[3]

A clear implication is that creativity is not solely the result of inherited genes. Learning certain skills and personality attributes must also play a role. At the present time, education in Western societies has swung toward content knowledge, and its evaluation by standardized tests. In Eastern societies, where content knowledge was prominent for centuries, a more equitable balance between the two goals is being sought. As research recently summarized in *Newsweek* reported, "Chinese student scores on an annual

---

[2] Shank & Cleary, 1995, p. 229.
[3] Zhao, 2011.

international assessment of creativity have been rapidly rising since 1990, whereas American scores have been decreasing. The test is considered valid by scholars, and has a high correlation with success later in life."[4]

The assessment referred to in that study[5] is based on the seminal work of psychologist E.P. Torrance.[6] He found that all ordinary creativity is characterized by four qualities: fluency, flexibility, originality, and elaboration. In the remainder of this chapter, because we believe Torrance's model remains the best available in this field, we present strategies that stimulate these four traits.

Fluency

Most creative thinking begins with generating ideas—lots of them. The emphasis is quantity, not quality. Freed from searching only for the "best" or "correct" answer, ideas flow from free-thinking, fast-moving thought processes. Later, of course, careful analysis of the most useful ideas will be necessary, but in the beginning, you should not worry about spelling, grammar, or how words are used.

ACTIVITY

11B

Brainstorming

Target age: 11 to 15
Goal: To generate as many ideas as possible
Materials needed: Paper and pencil
Script: This activity, though well known, continues to be unsurpassed as a stimulant to fluency. It is best done with two or more youth—the more the better. First, review the rules for brainstorming:

- Do not criticize the ideas of others. [Make a distinctive sound such as a beep if one of the children criticizes another's suggestion.]
- Don't edit your own ideas, either. "If you think it, say it!"

---

[4] "The Creativity Crisis," *Newsweek*, July, 2010.
[5] Kim, 2010.
[6] Torrance, 1995; Raina, 2000.

- Wild, funny, or even silly ideas are welcome.
- Produce as many ideas as you can.
- Build on what others have to say.
- Keep a record of your ideas.

I am going to ask you a question. You should think of as many answers as you can. Don't worry about being perfect. Don't worry about who goes first, or being called on. Just write down what you're thinking. The more answers you can think of, the better! What are all the uses you can think of for crayons?

After five minutes, have each participating child show or read his list. Then tell them to vote on and reveal the three ideas they feel are most useful. These votes are recorded where all can see. When all have reported, total the votes, and ask the children to discuss how this fluency activity could be changed to make it an even better way to solve problems.

Finally, present them with a new problem and allow them to engage in individual fluency. For example, why is it unfair to discriminate? You might want to read Dr. Martin Luther King's "dream" speech.

Adaptation for younger children: Although young children are familiar with crayons, it may be hard for them to think of suitable uses. They may do better with such non-specialized items as stones, bricks, or tin cans.

ACTIVITY

11C

Wandering Aimlessly

Wandering aimlessly around in an area of inquiry is often a good way to stimulate imagination. In order to wander, you have to be open to new things. You have to be willing to see what comes next in a problem or question, without overly controlling the objective of the search. In many schools throughout the world, the families of many of the students originally lived in other countries. For this exercise, let us imagine that the country is Brazil. Thus in this activity, your child will study the attractions of Brazil (or some other country) by looking through a variety of sources to learn more about it. As a result, she will be better able to think imaginatively about culture and diversity.

Target age: 6 to 10
Goal: To think of many ways that culture and social experience influence people's perceptions of places and regions
Materials needed: One of the following:

> *Countries of the World: Brazil* by Brian Dicks
> *Taking your Camera to Brazil* by Ted Park
> *Countries of the World: Brazil* by Zilah Deckker
> *A Visit to Brazil* by Peter and Connie Roop
> *Cultures of the World: Brazil* by Christopher Richard and Leslie Jermyn
> *We Come from Brazil* by Andre Lichtenberg
> A world map

Script: You and I are going to learn some interesting facts about Brazil, such as the primary language spoken, the country's various attractions, popular types of food, types of sports played, music, and dancing. In short, we will discover Brazil by virtually wandering around in the country, through reading one of these books that we will get from the library. I want you to ask questions about the Brazilian culture, and think of lots of reasons why it is important to learn about other people's cultures. Discover the location of the various sections of Brazil, so you can begin to discover how geography affects culture. The computer application called Google Earth can be most helpful here. You may want to create a travel brochure *filled* with interesting information and photos, so your friends can wander around Brazil, too.

Adaptation for older children: Being more skilled, older youth choose which country to study and can fulfill this assignment on their own.

Flexibility

The creative person is flexible in that she is open to the world, ready for change, and prepared to discover new ideas. She has the capacity to see the whole of a situation, rather than a group of uncoordinated details. Seeing all of the components in a problem, and not just fixating on one person, is much more likely to produce a creative solution. In high-pressure situations such as taking a test, most people seem to latch on to the first plausible idea they get and push it as far as they can. Creative thinkers always resist this tendency.

ACTIVITY

Metaphorical Thinking

A metaphor is a word or phrase that directly equates two things that aren't obviously alike. An instance would be, "The snow is a white blanket." As with analogies, the aim is to identify what is similar between the two concepts. If you were looking for a metaphor for a toothbrush, you might say it is "a tiny broom for sweeping your teeth clean." When Shakespeare wanted to suggest how it feels to be down on your luck he talked of "the slings and arrows of outrageous fortune."

It makes sense that there should be a relationship between creative thinking and metaphors. Using this figure of speech involves calling attention to a similarity between two seemingly dissimilar things. This is also often the case with creativity, and a growing body of research shows support for this relationship. For example, Howard Gardner, in his amazing book, *Art, Mind, and Brain,*[7] offers many insights into the process. He describes talking to a group of youngsters at a Seder (the meal many Jews eat to commemorate the flight of the Hebrews from Egypt). He told the children how, after a plague, Pharaoh's "heart was turned to stone." The children interpreted the metaphor variously, but only the older ones could understand the link between the physical universe (hard rocks) and psychological traits (a lack of feeling). Younger children are more apt to apply magical interpretations (God or a witch did it).

Target age: 11 to 15
Goal: Creating metaphors as a spur to creative thinking

---

[7] Gardner, 1995.

Materials needed: A book or website on the animal kingdom
Script: What are the different types of groups within the animal kingdom? The animal groups in this activity are mammals, reptiles, amphibians, birds, fish, and rodents. Here are brief definitions of the six groups:

- *Mammals* are animals that have hair, are warm-blooded, and nourish their young with milk.
- *Reptiles* are cold-blooded animals characterized by lungs, an outer covering of horny scales or plates, and young produced in eggs.
- *Amphibians* are cold-blooded, smooth-skinned animals that characteristically hatch as an aquatic larva with gills.
- *Birds* are warm-blooded, egg-laying, feathered animals, having forelimbs modified to form wings.
- *Fish* are cold-blooded aquatic animals having fins, gills, and a streamlined body.
- *Rodents* are warm-blooded mammals that have large incisors adapted for gnawing or nibbling.

You can learn more about the differences between them reading a brief article on zoology.

I want you to choose one of the groups of animals, then from within the class, I want you to pick a specific animal. Get to know more about your choice. Your goal is to make several metaphors about those animals.

Suppose you had chosen snakes. "She's a snake in the grass" would be a good metaphor. Another example might be, "He's a lion-hearted soldier." The goal is for you to understand your animal well enough so that you can come up with several different metaphors. This, in turn, will give you good practice in creative thinking.

Adaptation for older children: Have your child pretend to be the animal he has chosen. Is he happy or unhappy about his animal choice? In what ways is he like and unlike his animal? Might he be scared or proud to be that animal? One child we know responded: "I am a snake. I slither around looking for prey. I really like that I am predator to many other animals. It makes me feel somewhat safe and in control. I hope that I don't have to come across a crocodile, though. A crocodile is like a killing machine of the future—it could eat me!"

Originality

Perhaps the most crucial trait of creative thinkers is originality. Part of the reason they are original is that they have fluency and flexibility. However, they also are the ones who come up with ideas that nobody else thinks of. A major reason for this is that they possess a trait called "tolerance of ambiguity." Tolerant persons are able to welcome ideas that diverge from their own, and that attitude can be taught through practice. Such a person learns to willingly entertain original concepts, and often produces them.

We know a product is original only because we can compare it to norms to find it is rare. This is the case whether the product is a painting, a building, a formula, or an omelet. Take, for example, Salvador Dali's painting, *Crucifixion*.[8] The body of Christ is supported by cubes rather than bloody nails. Many viewers gasp when they turn a corner and look up for the first time.

ACTIVITY

Freedom of Function

Psychologists use the term "functional freedom" to denote the ability to see multiple uses for the objects you encounter. This is a creative trait, because you don't always have access to the right tool for a job, and will have to be inventive. This, too, increases your originality in the face of a problem you want to solve. People who have functional freedom enjoy the challenge of a thorny problem. They know from past experience that they often need to think of imaginative ways to approach problems. Not all their ideas will work, but they have faith that sooner or later, they will produce a good solution.

Target age: 6 to 10
Goal: More functional freedom, as a way to be more original
Materials needed: A large room or wide space outside under a close line. Two strings (9 feet long, or shorter if the ceiling of the room is less than 10 feet high), scotch tape, a tape measure, a mousetrap

---

[8]   See http://collections.glasgowmuseums.com/starobject.html?oid=1.

Script: Start by attaching the two strings to the ceiling of a 10-foot-high room, as in the drawing above. Each string is 9 feet long, and is firmly attached to the ceiling. If the room is less high, make the strings shorter accordingly. They are 14 feet apart, and there must be room for them to swing.

Your goal is simply to tie the two strings together. One item is available for your use in finding the solution—a mousetrap. Standing between the two strings, you should try to figure out how to tie the strings together, with or without the mousetrap. No matter how tall you are, you will not be able to reach the two strings, even if you try using the mousetrap to extend your reach. Do you think you can do it?

You might like to try this activity yourself before asking your child to try it.[9]

Adaptation for older and in children: Instead of the mousetrap, which most children find easy to attach to a string, use a screwdriver.

Many people are unable to reach this solution because they cannot imagine screwdrivers or mousetraps being used for something other than their usual purposes. Here's an example of what we mean: a graduate student in psychology studied the problem and said, "I've got it! The answer is the mousetrap. You catch a bunch of mice until you get one that isn't seriously hurt. You make a pet of it, then train it to be a 'trapeze' mouse. It will then jump up on one of the strings and swing back and forth until it is able to

[9]   The solution appears at the end of this chapter, on page 187.

swing over to you while you are holding the other string!" This is a good example of functional fixity: this student believed that a mousetrap could only be used to capture mice. His solution could conceivably work, but it is much more complicated than simply using the trap as a weight.

One young nun in John Dacey's class attempted to solve the problem. She decided that the mousetrap was really not necessary. Lifting the apron of her religious habit (the long formal dress nuns used to wear), she seized the over-sized rosary beads hanging from her belt. She swung them over her head while holding one of the strings, an amazing sight to behold! The beads caught onto the other string and, beaming with self-satisfaction, she tied in the strings together while those watching applauded! Although this is an imaginative method for solving the problem if you happen to be a nun, it wouldn't work for most of us.

Elaboration

Dr. Torrance once did a study of elaboration with first-graders.[10] Their creative abilities were measured by asking them to suggest how three toys could be improved to make them more fun to play with. The toys were a fire truck (considered a boy's toy), a nurse's kit (considered a girl's toy), and a stuffed dog (considered neutral at this age). The average scores broke down as would be expected: boys' scores were higher than girls' scores for the fire truck; girls' scores were similarly superior to those of boys on the nurse's kit; and the two sexes did about equally well with the stuffed dog. Torrance administered the same test two years later to the same children, when they were about to enter the third grade. The change was striking: boys were superior to girls on all of the toys, even the nurse's kit.

A number of explanations are possible. Perhaps girls simply become less creative with age. This seems unlikely, however, especially over such a short period of time. Torrance concluded that gender-role identification was the cause. He suggested that elementary school teachers (most of whom are female) teach young girls that they should behave according to the status quo. He stated than one can often hear teachers ask for "some strong boys to help me," while girls are more likely to be praised for being "lady-like." This study suggested that even when parents do not discourage creative imagination in girls, their elementary school teachers may do so.

[10]   Torrance, 1982.

ACTIVITY

Cotton Candy Clues

Years ago, a committee was tasked with thinking of ways to get rid of glass from junkyard cars. The metal was worth money, but the glass was worthless. To make a long story short, the solution came to one of the committee members while she was watching a cotton candy machine at a carnival. Suddenly it occurred to her that if the waste glass were melted, and sprayed against the side of a rotating cylinder, it could be turned into sheets of flexible material. That led to the invention of fiberglass.

Target age: 11 to 15
Goal: To apply lateral thinking techniques to quandaries
Materials needed: None
Script: Here is an exercise you can try which calls for adapting what's available. For example: *"What are all the uses you can think of for bricks?"* Some answers are:

- "Build a wall."
- "Build a house."
- "Build a fireplace."

Since these uses are what bricks are intended for, they do not exhibit much imagination. Here are other answers that do:

- Use a brick to write on a sidewalk.
- Use bricks as weapons to defend yourself if you are attacked.
- Use one as a funky paperweight.
- Most bricks are six inches long. Use one as a ruler.
- Use a brick to catch worms. Put one on a bare patch of ground, wait two weeks, and when you pick it up, there will be lots of worms under it!

Ask your child to suggest problems like this one. If she has trouble thinking of any, here are some examples you might suggest she try her hand at:

- What are all the implements you might use to remove a screw from a piece of wood, other than a screwdriver? [Pliers, table knife, nail clippers, etc.]
- How could you cook a meal if you were stuck for hours in a traffic jam during an evacuation? [Use one of your hub caps placed on the hot engine of your car, etc.]
- How would you move a very heavy wooden box? [Use a crowbar to winch it along; wedge round logs under it as rollers; attach it to a hot-air balloon to make it lighter, etc.]
- What would you use to start a fire if stuck in the woods during a snowstorm? [Use only branches still on trees; tear off bark strips from white birch trees, which burn even when totally soaked, etc.]

Adaptation for younger children: Employ simpler problems, such as uses for a pencil.

ACTIVITY

 11G

Huh?

Target age: 11 to 15
Goal: To think of ways to use lateral thinking to improve your child's problem-solving ability
Materials needed: None
Script: Can you think of reasonable answers to these questions?

1. How many sides does a circle have?
2. A truck driver is going down a one-way street the wrong way. A policeman looks over and waves a good morning to him. Why?
3. Take two apples from five apples and what do you have?

4. What is black when you buy it, red when you use it and grey when you throw it away?

5. If a farmer raises wheat in dry weather, what does she raise in wet weather?

[Lateral answers are given in the footnote below.[11]] Now, can you make your own puzzlers?

Adaptation for younger children: You might look for websites with easier puzzlers.

ACTIVITY

11H

Nearing Your Goal, Successively

Target age: 6 to 10

Goal: To elaborate on a theme as a way to gradually eliminate phobias

Materials needed: A picture of a snake; a 2-foot piece of hose or tubing; a toy rubber snake; and a real snake in a glass cage at your local zoo

While carrying out each of the following steps, your child should practice her favorite relaxation technique, and continue to do so until she reaches a calm state before proceeding to the next increment. As she does, you might present her with a small reward, making this reinforcement more powerful with each success.

1. I would like you to think about a snake. Can you picture it?
   [Relaxation exercise until pulse rate is about 75]
2. Now look at this picture of a snake.
   [Relaxation exercise until pulse rate is about 75]
3. Would you please handle this piece of hose.
   [Relaxation exercise until pulse rate is about 75]
4. Now do it while thinking about a snake.
   [Relaxation exercise until pulse rate is about 75]

---

[11] (1) Two sides. The inside and the outside. (2) He was walking. (3) You've got what you have taken—two apples. (4) Coal. (5) An umbrella.

5. Please spend some time handling this rubber snake while thinking about a real one.
   [Relaxation exercise until pulse rate is about 75]
6. Now we are going to the zoo where you look at a snake through the glass, without and then with a rubber snake in your hand.
   [Relaxation exercise until pulse rate is about 75]

If she is unable to calm down to a pulse rate about 75, repeat the step until she can. Ultimately she will be able to touch and handle a real snake.

Adaptation for older children: This same technique will probably work as well for them, but you might be able to go through the steps faster.

ACTIVITY

Lateral Thinking = Better Thinking

Target age: 10 to 15
Goal: To encourage your child to elaborate in imaginative, unique ways
Materials needed: None, but a minimum of two players is required
Script: A game that will help you to think laterally uses several common proverbs, such as "The apple doesn't fall far from the tree," "It takes one to know one," or "A bird in the hand is worth two in the bush." Think of as many of these adages as possible, and write down the first part of each one a 3″ by 5″ card. For example, you would write down "The apple doesn't fall …," "It takes one to …," or "A bird in the hand is worth …." The point of this game is to come up with funny endings. Put all your cards in a brown paper bag. Each player chooses a card from the bag and then has 15 seconds to come up with a different, funny ending for the saying. For example, if you pick "The apple doesn't fall …" you might come up with the ending " … if you're holding onto it really, really tight." After all the cards are used, discuss which of the endings each of you found the funniest.

Adaptation for younger children: Use nursery rhymes instead of adages. Read the first line of a nursery rhyme to your child, then have him make up the next line, using his own silly ideas.

You can find lots of strategies for fostering creative thinking on the Web. Now that you have some models to follow, we hope you will spend a lot of time nurturing your child's imagination. Our planet desperately needs you to do so!

Solution to page 181: Attach the mousetrap (or a screwdriver) to one of the strings, then swing it away from you. Go grasp the other string, and when the first string swings back to you, catch it. The two strings can then be tied together easily.

12

Thinking Critically and Wisely

Powerful emotions create strong memories; and memories, when coupled with language, are the basis for forming conscious beliefs. This level of belief is what we often call 'knowledge,' but if it doesn't have an emotional appeal, the belief will not register deeply in a person's mind.[1]

Throughout this book we have emphasized the importance of children knowing about themselves and how they feel about their own place in the world. Beyond simply knowing, it is even more important that your child has the confidence to reflect critically on situations he encounters. The term "critical thinking" is used often in current educational parlance—it refers to purposeful judgment and the ability to think clearly and rationally, especially when facing a conflict. What, then, is the opposite of critical thinking? Thinking murkily and irrationally? It might seem silly, but current educational practices in too many schools and classrooms around the planet tend to promote cautious, compliant memorization, as opposed to slow-paced, reflective thinking. This experience tends to leave many children feeling fuzzy-headed and uninspired. The emotional component of thinking, learning, and knowing should not,

[1] Newberg & Waldman, 2006.

Your Child's Social and Emotional Well-Being: A Complete Guide for Parents and Those Who Help Them, First Edition. John S. Dacey, Lisa B. Fiore, and Steven Brion-Meisels.
© 2016 John Wiley & Sons, Ltd. Published 2016 by John Wiley & Sons, Ltd.
Companion website: www.wiley.com/go/daceywellbeing

therefore, be ignored. When children enhance their social and emotional skills, their academic skills are enhanced as well.

It is not enough, then, to hope that children receive information that will prepare them for college, career, and life success. "Critical thinking is sterile without the capacity for empathy and comprehension that stretches the self."[2] Education, personal proclivities, biases, values, and motivations all contribute to a child's cognitive ability. In simple terms, critical thinking examines assumptions and biases (WHY?), discerns hidden values and evaluates evidence (WHAT?), and assesses conclusions (HOW?).

Critical thinkers:

- Ask pertinent questions.
- Assess statements and arguments.
- Are able to admit a lack of understanding or information.
- Have a sense of curiosity.
- Are interested in finding new solutions.
- Are able to clearly define a set of criteria for analyzing ideas.
- Are willing to examine their own beliefs, assumptions, and opinions and weigh them as objectively as possible.
- Listen carefully to others and give them clear-headed feedback.
- Suspend judgment until all the facts have been gathered and considered.
- Look for evidence to support assumptions and beliefs.
- Are able to adjust opinions when new facts are found.
- Reject information that is incorrect or irrelevant.
- See that critical thinking is a lifelong process of self-assessment.[3]

As children develop physically and cognitively, their brains change in fundamental ways. "The brain continues to 'prune' or cut down on connections between nerve cells, a process that is essential for the development of a complex system of logic." (Some researchers have concluded that the absence of this pruning is the basic cause of attention deficit disorder, as well as attention deficit hyperactive disorder.)[4]

Ideas with no purpose or benefit, as well as the neural feedback loops that support them, are systematically weakened and ultimately eliminated. Neural connections that support new, important beliefs are formed and strengthened. Practicing critical thinking helps children recognize analysis

[2]   Roth, 2010.
[3]   Paul & Elder, 2010.
[4]   Newberg & Waldman, 2006.

of ideas as a learning process, and not an end in itself. Thinking therefore becomes more than the act of memorizing facts and formulas—it requires expanding one's belief system, taking moderate risks, and recognizing elements that lead to new and deeper understandings.

Psychologist and author William James once wrote, "To perceive the world differently, we must be willing to change our belief system, let the past slip away, expand our sense of now, and dissolve the fear in our minds."[5] Over 100 years later, educator and author Ian Gilbert offers a similar recommendation: "Open minds to question, to reflect, to look beneath the surface, to have beliefs that they will fight for and fight for the beliefs of others, even if they don't agree with them."[6] The following activities are designed to promote making predictions based on information gathered. When your child is able to successfully discriminate among various facts and ideas, he will be better equipped to evaluate situations and make informed decisions.

Activities that Foster Recognition and Prediction

The activities in this section are aimed at your child's ability to use his five senses well. Recent research has even proposed additional senses, including proprioception (i.e., our awareness of our bodies and how they are situated in a spatial sense) and a vestibular (inner ear) sense that helps us stay balanced. To assist his ability to recognize and predict the truth, you can add your own creative flourishes and expand these activities.

ACTIVITY

Mystery Boxes

Target age: 6 to 10
Goal: To encourage your child to make predictions based on information he gains from using his senses. He will learn to look at and use data as scientists do

---

[5] James, 2007.
[6] Gilbert, 2014.

Materials needed: A few small boxes, such as 3″ × 5″ cardboard jewelry boxes, or boxes that can be recycled from home (such as those originally containing instant oatmeal packets, granola bars, or macaroni and cheese (if using recycled boxes, it is helpful to cover the boxes with construction paper or brown paper bag paper in order to make them look the same); an assortment of small objects such as buttons, paper clips, and/or pennies; tape.

Script: This activity can be done with one child or a small group of them. Before you begin the activity, prepare the boxes in advance so that each box contains one object or a few of the same objects inside. Tape each box closed securely so that no objects can fall out if the box is shaken. You may want to make several identical boxes if you will be sharing this activity with more than one child.

You will be using your senses to try and guess what objects are in each of these boxes. The senses that we each possess—sight, smell, sound, taste, touch—are needed to understand our world and ourselves.

I'm going to place one box in front of you. I want you to use your sense of sight to begin noticing features of the box. As you describe the box, notice the difference between what you actually see and what you infer. For example, "The box is a rectangle" and "It is blue" are observations. An inference would be something like, "Whatever is inside must be quite small." While observations can be supported by evidence and facts, inferences are not as clear, and can be arrived at through deducing from what you see.

Now that you have looked at the box and shared your thoughts about it, examine it by using your other senses. For example, you might shake the box and listen to the sound the object(s) make, or note how the object(s) feel being shaken inside the box.

After several different observations have been recorded, ask your child,

How about a prediction? What do you think is in the box? How do you know?

You can also ask your child how confident he is about the prediction.

Adaptation for older children: Older children can record their own observations on paper, without instructions about how to do it. They also can discuss their confidence in their conclusions, such as whether or not they'd feel comfortable presenting their predictions in front of their friends or classmates.

ACTIVITY

Character Bags

Target age: 6 to 10

Goal: To use clues to make connections between familiar objects and character traits

Materials needed: Paper lunch bags; household items that remind your child of favorite characters from books, television shows, or films; white paper; crayons, markers, or other materials for coloring; or your own electronic device

Script: This activity can be used with one child or small groups. The first few times you engage in this activity with your child, you can create the bags for him, and as he gains familiarity with the activity, he may want to prepare the bags for you to make the guesses, or for friends to guess different characters from the materials inside the bags. To begin, prepare bags in advance by thinking about favorite characters that your child knows from books, television shows, or films. Some examples are:

Harry Potter	Eloise	Winnie-the-Pooh
Curious George	Junie B. Jones	Max and Ruby
Arthur	Nancy Drew	Ms. Frizzle
Ramona	Berenstain Bears	Amelia Bedelia
Jack and Annie		
(*The Magic Tree House*)	Thomas the Tank Engine	
Flat Stanley	Percy Jackson	Katniss Everdeen

Select about five items from around the house that remind you of the specific character. For example, for Harry Potter you might include a picture of an owl, a miniature broom from a dollhouse, a pair of glasses, a small ball, a magic wand, or other related items that remind you of Harry Potter books and films. Repeat this with different bags so that you have several bags for your child to explore.

Choose one of these bags. Inside each bag you'll find different items. As you look at each item, think about what the object is, what it is typically used for, and notice what it reminds you of. All of the items in each bag connect to each other because they stand for a character in a book or movie, which is one of your favorites.

If your child has questions about a specific item or its function, feel free to provide extra clues or hints. Once he has figured out the correct character, ask him to draw a picture of the character, and then you or he can glue or tape the picture to the front of the paper bag and it will be complete. You can then have a display of all the different characters and their items, and you can return to them over time, or materials can be swapped and replaced. His thoughts and ideas about the characters might change over time as well.

Adaptation for older children: Instead of preparing the character bags for your child, let him prepare the bags for you to examine and guess which character the items represent.

ACTIVITY

You Complete Me

Target age: 6 to 10

Goal: To use visual clues and to recognize an image from an incomplete representation

Materials needed: Pictures from magazines or photocopies of illustrations from favorite books; construction paper; scissors; glue or tape; pencils, markers, and/or crayons for drawing

Script: To prepare this activity in advance, choose a picture from a magazine or a photocopy of an illustration from a favorite children's book. Cut out a section of the illustration so that, for example, two-thirds of the image remains but the middle section is now missing. Glue the newly altered illustration to a piece of paper. Show the piece of paper to your child.

What do you notice about this picture?

He will likely answer by telling you what the image represents. You should probe his thinking further to elicit more details about the image:

What kind of details do you see? How do you know it's a _____ if we don't see the whole _____? What would happen if you changed this into something else?

Give your child an opportunity to draw the missing part of the illustration. He can try to represent it as it actually is, or he can use his own creative touches to enhance the image and change it to his liking.

   Once he is finished, ask him about his choices:

Tell me about your idea(s). How did you decide to draw this _____?

Adaptation for older children: They might speculate about how the newly completed image would impact the story (if the image is from a favorite book) or the person or environment (if the image is from a magazine). Your child can practice making predictions based on the changes he makes with his drawings.

The activities above provide opportunities for your child to produce concrete information and evidence, and they also provide him with the freedom to create new understandings about the relationships. The activities that follow show how critical thinking helps us evaluate information through careful examination.

Activities that Foster Discernment

One of the benefits of being able to think critically is that it helps us avoid some common thinking errors or traps. These are ways of viewing situations through lenses that inevitably make us feel insecure. Being able to discern such situations accurately will help your child avoid falling into harmful habits of mind. Examples of these thinking traps include:

- *Telescopic vision.* Looking at things through one end or the other of the telescope makes them seem bigger or smaller than they really are.
- *Black-and-white thinking.* Looking at things in only extreme or opposite ways (e.g., good or bad, never or always, all or none).
- *Dark glasses.* Thinking about only the negative side of the matter.
- *Fortune-telling.* Making predictions about what will happen in the future without enough evidence.
- *Making it too personal.* Blaming yourself for things that aren't your fault.
- *Blame game.* Blaming others for things for which you should take responsibility.[7]

The following activities encourage your child to use his ability to discern clues, rules, and strategies that will give him an advantage in solving a problem. There are no correct answers to these challenges—only opportunities to generate more solutions.

ACTIVITY

Triangle Challenge

Target age: 11 to 15

Goal: To practice noticing features and perceiving boundaries

Materials needed: Triangle dot sheet (below); 2 different-colored pencils

Script: The goal of this activity is simple—to create as many triangles as possible by connecting the dots. You may choose to play this game with me, or you may want to play with a friend. We each take turns connecting two dots into a line. As lines are formed, we'll eventually create some triangles. If you connect the final line to form a triangle, then you can put the first letter of your name inside the triangle. If I [or one of your child's friends] am the one to complete the triangle, I [or the friend] put an initial in the middle of the triangle, and so on.

---

[7]   Merrell & Gueldner, 2010.

As you progress through the activity, you can encourage your child to think creatively. For example,

A triangle's sides need not only be three segments long. They could be 3 dots by 3 dots by 3 dots long, or 4 dots by 4 dots by 4 dots, and so on. The different colored pencils will help indicate who has discovered the many varying triangles. While it is certainly fun to see who establishes the most triangles, you should learn so much by seeing how creatively different triangles can be identified and how one person might see a triangle while the other doesn't.

Adaptation for younger children: Younger children can begin by connecting two dots at a time, and progressing to making triangles. If they are so inspired, and happen to be learning about different shapes, then squares, rectangles, and other shapes can be formed during this activity, bounded only by their imagination.

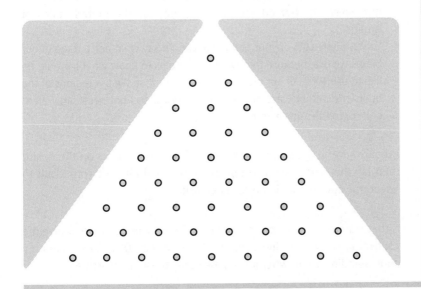

ACTIVITY

 12E

Fact or Opinion?

Target age: 6 to 10

Goal: To develop the ability to make decisions based on facts, rather than on assumptions or popular ideas

Materials needed: Index cards that have been prepared with prompts; blank cards; pencil/pen

Script: It's interesting to pause and think about how often our beliefs result from popular opinion or even false myths. Some examples of this include:

- Christopher Columbus discovered America (he actually wound up on various Caribbean islands and the coasts of Central and South America, but never set foot on the land we know as the United States of America).
- You use only 10% of your brain. (We cannot say what percentage of our brains we use, because that would require us to know what it would be like to use 100% of our brain. No one knows that. We use regions of the brain in different ways doing different tasks, and not necessarily all at once or to the same extent.)

Prepare several index cards with several such statements on them, and then lay the cards face down on the table or floor. Ask your child to select one and to read it aloud. Then ask,

Is that statement a fact or an opinion? How do you know? Now give me your reasons for believing your answer is correct. Okay, now here's my understanding about whether you are correct in your assessment.

If you find that you disagree about whether or not something is fact or opinion, there is a simple way to find out—is the statement something that can be tested and supported with evidence? Here are some examples that you may use:

- My teacher is the tallest teacher in the school.
- Gum that's chewed for two minutes is stickier than gum chewed for one minute.
- Dogs are friendlier than cats.
- My brother (or sister, or other family member) is heavier than your brother (or sister, or other family member).
- Red cars are more popular than gray cars.
- Exercise is good for your health.

Explain to your child some ways that might help him decide whether a statement is fact or opinion. This is the same process that scientists use to test their hypotheses (see Chapter 5), and that advertising companies use to generate interest in products. Ask:

How could you use these two ideas (facts and opinions) to help you make decisions?

Adaptation for older children: Older children can compare stories in the newspaper to Op-Ed pieces to see what they notice about the different ways that authors present their material.

The ability to discern fact from opinion has benefits that extend beyond avoiding getting suckered into purchasing a more expensive toy or game. Teaching your child the difference between fact and opinion will serve him well when he is faced with choosing whether or not to smoke cigarettes, get into a car driven by a friend who has been drinking, or vote for a classmate running for school office. Thinking outside he proverbial box is precisely what consultants do when hired by companies that are stuck in a rut. Consultants are paid to:

- Ask the right questions.
- Identify needs, strengths, and weaknesses.
- Help answer those needs and solve problems.
- Provide tools and useful advice.
- Describe steps to improve performance.
- Boost satisfaction and motivation.[8]

[8] Gurr, 2013.

ACTIVITY

Thunk

Opportunities for children to stretch their thinking and discern multiple angles in a situation are, unfortunately, not as common as opportunities to follow directions and rules in school. In response to this phenomenon, Ian Gilbert created what he calls "Thunks."[9] These are statements that provoke thinking and reflection. The examples below are a terrific way to transition into the next assortment of activities for you and your child. These types of thinking exercises provide the mental calisthenics that help your child keep his reasoning sharp:

- If science can't prove something works, does it not work even if it works?
- If you turn a speaker upside down does the music come out upside down, and is it the same for the light when you turn a torch upside down?
- Do flames have sides?
- Would an iPod with one track on it work in "shuffle" mode?
- Does your dog know what it did last summer?
- Does a room weigh more if it has a strong smell in it?

Activities that Promote Ethical Reflection

Provocations like those presented above encourage your child to think about *why* something is so, not just the *what*. This kind of deep understanding, further explored in the activities below, allows children to better analyze and articulate differing viewpoints.

---

[9]   Gilbert, 2014.

ACTIVITY

What Kind of Water Are You?

Target age: 6 to 15

Goal: To encourage your child to think about qualities that reflect the whole of him—his being in terms of physical, social, emotional, and other attributes

Materials needed: None

Script: If you had to choose, would you say you are more like a lake, an ocean, or a waterfall?

Some children may not be familiar with each of these bodies of water, and if that is the case finding pictures in a book or a search on the computer will yield examples that they can explore. As your child discusses his thinking about which he is—lake, ocean, or waterfall—see which qualities he chooses to highlight in his explanation. These qualities may be ones that you also perceive. Some, however, may be ones you don't readily associate with your child's behavior, appearance, or intellect. These provide excellent opportunities for conversation about the qualities we have and those we wish we had.

For example, the fact that a lake is often still may be viewed by some people as calm and peaceful, while others may view that stillness as boring or limited. Some people may perceive oceans as wild and unpredictable, and others may perceive them as controlled by gravitational pull of the moon. All of these make for rich, stimulating discussion and self-reflection for your child and you.

ACTIVITY

Just One Rule

Target age: 6 to 10
Goal: To consider the consequences of decision-making in establishing rules
Materials needed: Paper and pencil/pen; your own electronic device
Script: You've probably found yourself in a situation when you thought something you wanted to do was reasonable, but instead you were told you couldn't do it because it was against the rules or not allowed. Some rules are clearly established to prevent injury or other harm, but there are some rules that simply don't seem to make sense. And yet the person in power has the authority to adhere to the rules or make an exception based on the circumstances. What do you wish would happen?

For children at different ages, rules take on different meanings as they attempt to make sense of the world. For a 6-year-old, the rules in Monopoly aren't as important as they are to a 9-year-old, who might vehemently argue his stance on owning Park Place and collecting $200 when he passes "Go." A 15-year-old, on the other hand, won't care so much about making allowances as long as there is some general sense of fairness for all players.

Suppose you have the chance to make up one rule that everyone in the world will have to follow. What is the rule that you would choose?

Once your child has shared his rule, continue:

Let's think about the implications of your rule. Why did you choose this rule? How do you think it would affect other kids? What difference would it make in the lives of adults? Do you think most people would be happy that you want to have that role?

A lot of discussion and debate about the effects of your child's rule is likely to occur, especially about how it could potentially help and hinder people.

Adaptation for older children: Older children can be asked to think of rules or laws throughout history that have been made and how they have affected people (for example, the Dred Scott decision of the Supreme Court). You can ask your child if he notices trends, such as certain groups being privileged or oppressed.

ACTIVITY

 12

Easy Come, Easy Go

Target age: 11 to 15
Goal: To encourage your child to think about what it means to want something, to lose something, and to consider the actions of giving and receiving, all through an ethical lens
Materials needed: None
Script: Speak with your child about the idea of having three wishes. This is a common theme in many folk tales, such as *The Fisherman and His Wife* by the Brothers Grimm and the story of Aladdin in *One Thousand and One Nights* (a.k.a. *Arabian Nights*). If he isn't familiar with these stories, they are readily available in books found at the library or online.

You can have any three things that you wish for, but in exchange you must give away three things. What would you ask for, and what would you give away?

This is an opportunity to learn more about your child's cares, concerns, and values, as well as his opinions about fairness, equity, and sacrifice. As you discuss these ideas with your child, see what themes come up in conversation. You may want to ask your child some follow-up questions about his choices. For example,

How do your choices compare with what you'd have expected your friends to say? What memories come up for you about your previous behavior?

> *Adaptation for younger children*: Younger children can benefit from reading one of the books mentioned above with you, or watching a video or film version of the story. Once your child is familiar with the story, you can have a discussion about fairness, equality, power, oppression, and other themes as you or he are so inspired.

Researchers argue that citizens need to make our schools more like learning gymnasia, rather than the old assembly line and monastery models that are still so frequently to be found. The gymnasium analogy involves developing children's learning stamina and stretching their learning muscles. Similar to any successful fitness plan, strengthening your child's learning stamina and muscles will have short-term gains and long-term benefits so that, ultimately, he will do more than simply perform better on standardized assessments. He will be a confident, curious, motivated learner for the rest of his life.

This chapter opened with a quote that emphasized the role of emotions in forming knowledge, which contributes to the formation of our own belief systems and, eventually, wisdom. As any parent knows, what you may consider "best" for your child may not be readily embraced by him. There is almost always an emotional component that contributes to an intellectual decision. One author summed up this experience by recounting his own childhood experience of being persuaded by his mother to eat his peas:

Today, I continue to treat the world as an interconnected whole, where everyone and everything has value and a place and is to be treated with equal kindness and respect. And it all began with a series of childhood beliefs: the belief that you have to listen to your parents (at least some of the time); the belief that vegetables are good for you (at least some of the time); and the belief—which was triggered by an overwhelming feeling of guilt— that peas had feelings and friends ... The emotional experience associated with eating peas induced one of the earliest moral beliefs of my childhood: peas are fundamentally evil. The fact that somebody else tells you they are good for you is not enough to override the emotional desire to throw them across the room...[10]

In the chapter that follows, we present strategies for you to get help with your efforts to strengthen your child's social and emotional development.

---

[10]   Newberg & Waldman, 2006.

Part VI

Achieving Your Goals Even More Effectively

13

Getting Help with Your Efforts

"Being mindful of oneself as a community member becomes part of knowing oneself. The community must be a healthy, vibrant place if it is to have the role of eliciting good and true ideas and actions from its members."[1]

Seitel's statement reinforces that of anthropologist Margaret Mead: "Never doubt that a small group of thoughtful, committed citizens can change the world; indeed it's the only thing that ever has." How you define community may differ from what your neighbor, congressional representative, and even your spouse may think. What matters most, however, is that you feel supported in your own efforts as you work, lovingly and consistently, to enhance your child's well-being.

You've spent significant time and energy focusing on ways to help strengthen your child's social and emotional skills. This investment reflects your commitment to your child. Nevertheless, the factors affecting a person's growth are tremendously complex. None of us functions in isolation, so we need to identify the supports available to us. We also benefit from recognizing our own humanity and limitations. Parents and caregivers receive much criticism, praise, and advice (solicited and unsolicited). There is soci-

---

[1] Seitel, 2009, p. 91.

Your Child's Social and Emotional Well-Being: A Complete Guide for Parents and Those Who Help Them, First Edition. John S. Dacey, Lisa B. Fiore, and Steven Brion-Meisels.
© 2016 John Wiley & Sons, Ltd. Published 2016 by John Wiley & Sons, Ltd.
Companion website: www.wiley.com/go/daceywellbeing

etal pressure to achieve, but not be too successful, and to know the difference! Noted psychologist Ned Hallowell writes, "Good parents often do too much for their children. This is their one great mistake. And its corollary mistake is that they (I should say, we) don't say 'No!' enough … But I also [know] how hard we parents can work to provide joy rather than letting our kids learn how to create it."[2]

The message here is to let go of the guilt that many of us parents feel when we don't indulge our children, or when we don't know how to fix every problem. There is much to be gained from guiding children along their developmental paths, but also much to be gained from getting out of the way once in a while. Psychologist Shefali Tsabary writes:

> As parents, we may feel guilty if we put our needs on a par with our children's. We may feel ashamed to ask for time and space for ourselves, independent of our children. If they watch us constantly sidestep ourselves, perhaps by sacrificing our own needs for those of our spouse or friends, they will learn to devalue themselves in favor of others. … For this reason, we do our children a spiritual service when we develop our own ability to fulfill ourselves and take care of our emotions on our own.[3]

The focus of this chapter is to provide you with concrete actions that you can take to gain support for your goals. Instead of activities, you are presented with suggested actions that will connect you with:

- People in similar positions – parents, caregivers, and teachers.
- Practitioners working in school contexts.
- National organizations striving to advance children's social and emotional well-being.
- Additional resources to further your own learning and share with others.

Support for Caregivers and Teachers

The following actions encourage you to form relationships with friends, neighbors, and other community members as you continue to shape strategies that will enhance your child's social and emotional learning.

---

[2] Hallowell, 2002, p. 222.
[3] Tsabary, 2010, p. 180.

ACTION

Find a Buddy

While every parent has her own set of circumstances and respon-sibilities, there are many experiences that parents share, such as feelings of uncertainty and doubt in their own abilities. For example, if your child has been diagnosed with specific physical, cognitive, or behavioral challenges, then your own feelings of insecurity, frustration, and sadness will almost certainly be heightened. It is important to recognize that you are not alone in your parenting experience. When you are able to form connections with others, you will notice that the intensity of many feelings and concerns decreases.

One of the most obvious sources for support and validation is other parents. They have often been through similar situations that you are experiencing and are therefore a vital source of support, including tis-sues and laughter. A relationship with even one other parent is all that it takes to reduce your own anxiety.

There are many opportunities to meet other parents, including groups inside and outside the school community. The following online organizations provide information about local opportunities for par-ents and caregivers to get involved:

Moms Club
Website: www.momsclub.org
Originally created as a source of support for stay-at-home moms, this club is now international.

Work it, Mom!
Website: http://workitmom.com
While not limited to working mothers, this group was specifically developed to address the many challenges encountered by working moms.

Dads Move
Website: www.dadsmove.org
Provides resources and face-to-face support groups for dads.

Fathers Forum
Website: www.fathersforum.com
  Features social networks and face-to-face and online resources aimed at fathers.

The Handsome Father
Website: www.thehandsomefather.org
  Provides gay fathers with a community, face-to-face and online. The organization provides listings of support groups and networking opportunities, as well as mentorship and resources to fathers in different stages of parenting.

Family Equality Council
Website: www.familyequality.org/get_involved/parent_groups/
  Offers a listing of local resources for parents to use to connect with each other in person and online.

If you are inspired to begin your search for a support network in your local community, some places to look are:

- Your child's school's parent–teacher organization or association (PTO/PTA).
- Your local public library.
- Your child's pediatrician or a local hospital.
- A local faith-based organization.
- An existing group for a specific diagnosis/disability.

Often, town or city halls have resources at the ready for new residents, so even if you have lived in your community for years and are only now interested in exploring new avenues for connections as a parent, this is an excellent place to start. If you feel dissatisfied with the options that you uncover in your search, then start your own support group! The actions that follow suggest some choices that will help you in this effort.

ACTION

Form a Parents Support Group

One of the quickest ways to get connected to others is by asking, "How can I help?" For example, a local PTA wanted to raise funds to purchase a set of benches in the school's library. The group was struggling to find the money and connect with parents, until one mom – new to the school community – asked if she could provide help. In a short time she was provided with class lists, names of fellow parents, and community members (e.g., business leaders, builders) who had expressed a desire to contribute. This opportunity provided the new mom with almost instant contacts and a reason for connecting that she might have otherwise felt awkward about.

We sometimes do not notice how much we rely on others for many different things – big and small. Being able to help others very often results in helping oneself:

- Establish a network of responsible, reliable babysitters/childcare providers.
- Form playgroups for children at different ages.
- Connect adults in social events (e.g., BBQs, yard sales, block parties).
- Inspire advocacy and activism for specific local causes.

For detailed tips and guidelines for starting your own local support group, see the Edmodo website (www.edmodo.com). If you have access to online resources, either from home or from a computer at a public library, for example, you will find yourself at a tremendous advantage when it comes to connecting with others. There are seemingly boundless resources available online. The actions below will guide you in getting started, and will lessen any initial anxiety about it.

ACTION

Find Online Support

Thanks to the numerous social networking sites that currently exist, such as Facebook, Twitter, and Instagram, many parent support groups exist solely online. Such groups provide forums for parents to come together around one or more common interests, regardless of geographical location, and offer rich opportunities for sharing ideas, advice, and resources.

Many websites feature discussion and/or messaging boards so that visitors to the site can discuss information, concerns, and opinions. These boards range from those that function like bulletin boards, where visitors post messages that others can see (one-way communication) to discussion forums that occur in *asynchronous* or *synchronous* fashion. An asynchronous discussion forum means that visitors can post comments or questions at any time, and someone can respond at another time. Participants do not need to be online at the same time in order to view, post, or respond. Synchronous discussion forums occur at specific times, and participants can post and respond in the moment, sometimes bringing people into contact from around the world.

The following sites are popular places for parents and others to explore, and do not require any fees for the use of their platforms:

Facebook
Website: www.facebook.com
Once you have established a free Facebook account, you can look to the "Groups" link on the left-hand menu. There are icons to "Create Group" and "Find New Groups," and you are able to adjust your privacy settings (e.g., who can see your personal information) by clicking on the icon that looks like a padlock with three little lines. The site is very user-friendly, and there are also many online tips available outside of the Facebook site for those who have the time and inclination to explore the Internet for Facebook-inspired ideas.

Pinterest
Website: www.pinterest.com
This site functions like an interactive bulletin board, allowing users to "pin" websites to their own accounts. For example, suppose you search for "healthy snacks" and find a recipe for creative after-school snacks. To save this recipe, you can "pin" it to your "board." You are able to create your boards, almost like file folders, where your different pinned websites are available as snapshots for you to look at. When you wish to access the specific site, such as the recipe, all you need to do is click on the pinned image and you will be taken directly to the desired website. You are also able to "follow" friends and others on Pinterest, and can therefore connect with others around specific interests or activities. There are numerous sites to explore related to parenting on Pinterest, featuring tips, humor, and forums for exchange.

Edmodo
Website: www.edmodo.com
This site is specifically designed to bring teachers, families, and students together in the spirit of sharing. It is particularly useful for professionals – teachers and administrators who are interested in advancing their goals for their school community and/or the broader school district. Featuring support in the form of videos, webinars, and other resources, Edmodo is a secure website that offers many opportunities for engagement. A detailed set of instructions walks users through the process of connecting with others on a specific topic or for continued professional development.

Creating a bridge between the home and school environments helps support children's successful development. The section that follows presents more information about the school context as a place for strengthening children's social and emotional skills.

Actions that Create Support in the School Context

Most efforts to strengthen social and emotional skills in schools are designed to include all students, even though 80% of typical school populations do not have mental health problems. Nevertheless, experts have argued that the most successful attempts to increase resiliency and social competence in school settings include SEL programs. They also involve protective factors, such as "a positive and caring school climate, development of positive relationships between students and their teachers, and effective academic instructional planning."[4] The underlying idea here is one of synergy, where two interventions delivered simultaneously – in the home and in the school –have greater impact.

The following actions encourage connections between the home and school environments. Working collaboratively, you can enhance your child's social and emotional skills in general.

ACTION

13D

Building School Support

Developing trust, promoting a caring community that welcomes and respects differences, fostering cooperation and companionship, and otherwise creating a humane climate – these are all goals that most schools support. Furthermore, the majority of schools engage in ongoing self-evaluation to see how well the school is meeting these goals.

One of the ways parents can reach out to school administrators and teachers is simply by showing up – making an appointment for a face-to-face meeting or a phone call if meeting during a typical workday isn't possible. These initial meetings provide opportunities for parents and school staff to:

- Get to know each other.
- Explore shared interests and goals.
- Establish shared priorities for the school.
- Focus efforts on SEL.

Also, administrators need to work with teachers to integrate SEL principles and strategies. Setting high expectations for students, staff, and

---

[4]   Merrell & Gueldner, 2010, pp. 104–105.

families is a means of expressing care. Many school districts throughout the world have articulated SEL as a priority in combating threats to
their communities.[5] A recent publication of the International Academy of
Education (IAE), an organization that offers "timely syntheses of research-
based evidence of international importance," features the statement:

> Indeed, schools worldwide must give children intellectual and practical
> tools they can bring to their classrooms, families and communities.
> Social-emotional learning provides many of these tools. It is a way of
> teaching and organizing classrooms and schools that help children
> learn a set of skills needed to manage life tasks successfully, such as
> learning, forming relationships, communicating effectively, being
> sensitive to others' needs and getting along with others.[6]

As an engaged caregiver, your efforts may include bringing organizations such as the IAE to the attention of educational decision-makers
and the general public in your community. Educated citizens' votes
and actions can make a real difference in the lives of children.

Actions that Generate Support from External Resources

The following actions to will help you gain support from resources outside
of your community.

ACTION

13E

National and International Organizations

As you explore these organizations, you will find that you are drawn
to some because of their mission statements, and to others because of
their resources. Whatever resonates with you is a terrific place to start.

---

[5]   CASEL, 2014.
[6]   Elias, 2003.

Collaborative for Academic, Social, and Emotional Learning
Website: www.casel.org
Twitter: @caselorg
The leading organization in the United States for promoting SEL in preschool through high school, CASEL bases its advice entirely on evidence obtained in highly rigorous, widely respected research studies. The organization focuses its efforts and impact on research.

ASCD: The Whole Child
Website: www.ascd.org
Twitter: @ASCD
The Association for Supervision and Child Development is an international presence in curriculum development, designed to empower educators, promote leadership, and support success for individual and group learners.

UNICEF
Website: www.unicef.org
Twitter: @UNICEF
UNICEF is an organization dedicated to protecting the rights, health, and well-being of children around the world. It places particular emphasis on the early childhood years and children in the most vulnerable settings. Providing support across a range of contexts, from advocacy efforts to vitamin drops, UNICEF is committed to improving the lives of all children.

UNICEF has commissioned a document called The Rights Of Children. It is made up of numerous articles. Here, for example, is Article 18:

> Parental responsibilities; state assistance: Both parents share responsibility for bringing up their children, and should always consider what is best for each child. Governments must respect the responsibility of parents for providing appropriate guidance to their children – the Convention does not take responsibility for children away from their parents and give more authority to governments. It places a responsibility on governments to provide support services to parents, especially if both parents work outside the home.[7]

---

[7] UNICEF, 2015.

National Center on Safe & Supportive Learning Environments
Website: safesupportivelearning.ed.gov
Twitter: @SSLearn
The NCSSLE addresses issues such as bullying, harassment, violence, and substance abuse in an effort to improve learning conditions for all students. Funded by the U.S. Department of Education, this organization provides training to students, teachers, communities and families, and administrators at various levels.

Character Education Partnership
Website: character.org
Twitter: @CharacterDotOrg
This nonprofit organization envisions young people everywhere as educated, inspired, ethical, engaged citizens. Offering training, a national conference, and evaluation tools, the organization strives to connect educators and others who seek to improve school conditions.

Six Seconds
Website: www.6seconds.org
Twitter: @6s_EQ
Six Seconds reaches people across the globe who are engaged in efforts to teach emotional intelligence skills. This organization helps children, families, schools, and other groups to succeed.

National Parent-Teacher Association
Website: www.pta.org
Twitter: @NationalPTA
For over 100 years, National PTA has been recognized as the premier organization that connects stakeholders in children's educational experiences – families, students, teachers, administrators, and community members – with the shared goals of educational success for all learners and sustained, meaningful family involvement in schools. The work of the National PTA and its partners is promoted through publications, conferences, and social media venues.

National Institute of Mental Health
Website: www.nimh.nih.gov
Twitter: @NIMHgov

Dedicated to transforming the understanding and treatment of mental illnesses, this national organization supports and disseminates research on a variety of topics. Scientific perspectives and applications of numerous findings are presented in links to publications, blogs, and video clips.

National Association of School Psychologists
Website: nasponline.org
Twitter: @nasponline
This organization strives to empower school psychologists by promoting effective practices in the areas of advocacy, leadership, and cultural responsiveness.

ACTION

Publications

Many of the organizations listed above provide links to publications and resources that you may find useful and want to share with friends, relatives, and community members. The following resources offer additional information in a variety of formats – books, research articles, webinars, and podcasts. We encourage you to explore these websites, as each site offers publications that extend the conversation about children's social and emotional well-being.

The Inner Resilience Program
Website: http://www.innerresilience-tidescenter.org/publications.html

Defending the Early Years
Website: http://deyproject.org/recommended-reading-and-resources/

Schools that Learn
Website: http://schoolsthatlearn.com

Mindful Schools
Website: www.mindfulschools.org

As someone committed to children's social and emotional well-being, you recognize that the investment in children is effort that yields immeasurable short- and long-term rewards. Psychologist Shefali Tsabary advises parents:

> You need to teach your children to be unafraid of owning their voice, their space, and their needs. They thrive when they feel free to defend their rights. At the same time, they need to be able to give to others. True giving, which is fundamentally different from giving because it fills an empty space in your life and is therefore a form of neediness, comes from awareness of inner abundance. There is no giving if the inner well is dry. Authentic giving originates from a well that overflows.[8]

It is in this spirit that the chapters in this book are designed to fill your "well" and increase your own sense of "being." The chapter that follows provides a peek at what the future of social-emotional learning looks like for parents and practitioners.

---

[8] Tsabary, 2010, p. 181.

14

The Future of SEL

The beginnings of a tidal wave of support for SEL can be discerned in scholarly journals, professional blogs, newspaper articles, on the agenda of parent–teacher organizations, and in conversations along the sidelines at school sports events. Burgeoning interest may be discovered at all grade levels. The call for educational change is becoming universal.[1] Here are some of the changes which we believe are making the future of SEL so positive.

Greater Importance of SEL

Interest is being generated as SEL is seen to be more important. That is because:

- SEL will be recognized as being more responsible for success in life than academic learning (AL, which is composed of facts and methodologies).
- When students experience a deficit in SEL, whether due to lack of opportunity to learn or because of psychopathology, they will inevitably suffer a deficit in AL. Educational leaders will insist on a more reasonable balance between the two.

[1] Most of the predictions offered in this chapter are based on the opinions of experts in the field. The rest result from educated suppositions on our part.

Your Child's Social and Emotional Well-Being: A Complete Guide for Parents and Those Who Help Them, First Edition. John S. Dacey, Lisa B. Fiore, and Steven Brion-Meisels.
© 2016 John Wiley & Sons, Ltd. Published 2016 by John Wiley & Sons, Ltd.
Companion website: www.wiley.com/go/daceywellbeing

- Most teachers will realize that they became professional educators more because they care about SEL than because they care about AL. Most will begin to act on their distaste for "teaching to the test" and drilling children on facts.
- The majority of parents will come to see and understand that scores on the SAT tests correlate only with socioeconomic level. Such scores have little relation either to success in college(!) or success in life(!!).
- As a result, college admissions officers will deemphasize quantitative measures such as SATs and school grades, and will find ways to assess potential students' social and emotional skills, which do predict superior performance in college and in life.
- The power of SEL will be examined not only from the standpoint of psychology, sociology, and educational theory. It will also be studied from the physical viewpoint: the human hormonal and central nervous systems.
- The analysis and improvement of school social climate has become a popular topic for study. The environment in classrooms will continue to receive attention, which will in turn benefit SEL.
- The continued growth of family and school alliances will foster the success of SEL.
- SEL will find its way into college classrooms, especially those in the helping professions such as psychology and sociology.
- It will also begin to move into the curricula of graduate programs, most especially medicine, business, and education.[2]

Facilitation of SEL Goals

- Because, understandably, "if it's not tested, it's not taught," teacher assessment will devote a much more significant role to the evaluation of, and the educator's ability to foster, SEL.
- The measurement of SEL will be based on a combination of tests presented and scored by human and by computers. Groups of scholars are working on this aspect right now. The table below presents strategies that already exist. Although the two types of strategies (human and computer) can be equally valid and reliable, computers have the distinct advantage of being much less expensive to use. It is likely that in the near future electronic devices for this purpose will be available to all students, regardless of the economic state of the school system.[3]

---

[2] Goleman, 2005.

Types of in-school SEL measurement[3]

Type of measurement	Instrument name	Source	Age range	Cost	Human scoring	Computer scoring
1. Direct behavioral observation	Teacher judgement		3–18	High	Do not recommend	Do not recommend
2. Behavior rating scales	1. DESSA - DEvereaux Student Strengths Assessment	.kaplanco.cm	6–15	Mod.	Teachers, parents	Machine scorable
	2. Social-Emotional Assets and Resilience Scales (SEARS)	strongkids.uoregon.edu	3–18		Teachers, parents, strings	
3. Self-report instruments	1. Behavioral and Emotional Rating Scale–Second Edition (BERS-2)	proedinc.com	3–18	Mod.	Teachers, parents, students	Machine scorable
	2. Emotional Quotient Inventory (EQ-i®) -YV	mhs.com/eihc.aspx?id=WhatIsEI	6–18		Students	
			5–13		Students	
4. Sociometric techniques	1. Remote Associates test, A and B Seymor Mednick	remote-associates-test.com	A = 6–13, B = 14–18	Mod.	Do not recommend	Machine scorable
	2. Two-string test A. Maslow	See above	6–18			Machine scorable
	3. Fill in X's M. Ronco	See above	3–18			Machine scorable
5. Projective/ expressive techniques	Draw-a-family, ink blot		3–18	High	Do not recommend	Do not recommend
6. Interview techniques			3–18	High	Do not recommend	Do not recommend
7. Essay evaluation			3–18	$0	Do not recommend	Keyword search
8. Fluency of examples, e.g. # of instances of self-control			3–18	$0	Count with excellence rating	Example count
9. Instances of criminal behavior, e.g., weapons found			3–18	$0	Count with severity rating	Example count

3 Compiled by Dacey, 2015.

(Continued)

Types of in-school SEL measurement (*Continued*)

Type of measurement	Instrument name	Source	Age range	Cost	Human scoring	Computer scoring
10. Antisocial behavior counts, e.g., verbal fights				$0	School reports by classroom	School reports by classroom
11. Analyses of drawings: counting and pattern recognition	See Walt Haney, Boston College	Haney, Russell, & Bebell, 2004	3–18	$0	Haney, et al. – work-shop 1/22	???
12. School attendance records by classroom				$0	Do not recommend	Tallies of change in daily school attendance, after-school clubs and sports participation, pep rallies, etc.
13. Teacher inputs			3–18	$0	Documen-tation of use of SEL materials in classroom	Do not recommend
14. Shadow benefits	See Belfield et al., 2015	Columbia's Center for Benefit-Cost Studies: http://cbcse.org/	3–18	Mod.	Reduction in societal costs directly resulting from SEL	Reduction in societal costs directly resulting from SEL
15. School satisfaction survey	Organizational climate? Well-being?			$0–Mod.	Do not recommend	School, classroom-specific
16. Qualitative formative assessment	See Richards, R., Edutopia, 3/24/15	edutopia.org/blog/qfat-document-learning-mobile-technology-				

- The integration of SEL into the regular curriculum will occur mostly through infusing SEL strategies into regular AL requirements. It is possible that this will also be done, to a lesser extent, by reducing some AL requirements to make room for SEL. Here's an example of what we mean:

In a Spanish Harlem second grade class, I watched a session of "breathing buddies," part of the daily routine. One by one, each child took a small stuffed animal from a cubby, found a place to sit down, and put the animal on his or her belly. Then the children watched the animals go up on their in-breath, counting 1-2-3-4-5, and down on their out-breath, to the same count. This exercise, the teacher said, leaves them calm and focused for the rest of the day – a state sometimes hard to imagine given the tumultuous home lives typical of the housing project next to the school, where most of the second graders live.[4]

Return of the Arts

STEM (science, technology, engineering, and mathematics) is currently seen in most school systems as a unified subject matter area. In the future it will be known as "STEAM," with the A standing for the arts, such as drawing, art history, music, and drama. There will be teachers who specialize in the arts, and they will emphasize the role of SEL. In addition, the effect of studying the arts on other STEM subjects will become apparent. For example, those who do well in geometry will find they are better at dancing, and vice versa.

Online SEL

Electronic devices of all kinds will become as ubiquitous as blackboards and chalk used to be. These devices will make possible the cultivation of SEL through such complex methodologies as simulated reality and artificial intelligence. Less complex technologies such as video clips, online idea boards, and electronic games will also become more popular. Innovative

---

[4] Goleman, 2005, p. 594.

strategies may include new video games such as *The Sims* for boys, virtual friendship movies, such as *Hunger Games,* and religion-specific programs such as *OWL* (*Our Whole Lives,* for teaching sexuality values). Most likely the major concern will be the repercussions of too much use of electronics: "everyone connected, all the time."[5]

Non-Classroom Settings for SEL

Much imaginative instruction will begin to take place outside of classrooms but within schools. For example, after school, weekend, and summertime programs will be held on school property.[6] Some of this education will occur in camp-like settings, such as Project Adventure ropes courses, creativity projects, moral judgment exercises, sociodrama, and the showing of inspirational movies. Another innovation will be awards for actions that demonstrate social and emotional excellence. Students will be instructed that when they see especially humane behavior, they should report it to school authorities who will reward it.

Non-School Settings for SEL

Some SEL will take place in settings other than school properties altogether. For example, infant assessments of social and emotional abilities will take place in clinics, so that young children who suffer deficits can receive remedial care. Formal mediation of actual student–student and teacher–student disputes will be held, preferably in non-school settings.

More Caring Citizens

As we have noted elsewhere in this book, there is evidence of a decline in the average person's caring for his fellow citizens. In particular, we have seen a world-wide waning of college-student interest in civic responsibility. As the numbers of human beings have burgeoned, especially in the biggest of our cities, our caring for each other has dropped, perhaps as a defensive mechanism.

---

[5] Kurzweil, 2012, p. 21.
[6] Dacey, 1980.

It is tremendously important that this be rectified. We believe this will be one of the top priorities of future SEL. As Daniel Goleman puts it, "Recent studies suggest that the mammalian brain circuitry for caring, on which empathic concern depends, can be strengthened with the right training and that this, in fact, makes children kinder and more generous to others."[7]

More Research

There is one more area that we think will benefit SEL greatly: government- and privately funded research. As we have pointed out in numerous places in this book, there is a growing consensus among instructional leaders, activist parents, and indeed the general public. The whole world needs to do a better job of fostering SEL, and that will mean carefully controlled experiments and evaluations. Throughout the twentieth and so far in the twenty-first centuries, huge amounts of money have been spent on how to promote academic learning. Although SEL has suffered from an almost complete dearth of such support, we feel confident that this is about to change significantly. And as it does, we sincerely hope and believe that the universal yearning for the twin prospects of peace and prosperity will grow with it.

[7]   Goleman, 2005, p. 593.

References

AACAP. (2011). *Facts for Families Guide: Bullying.* At http://www.aacap.org/AACAP/Families_and_Youth/Facts_for_Families/FFF-Guide/Bullying-080.aspx

ADAA (Anxiety and Depression Association of America). (2013). Blog on treatment. At adaa.org/blog/anxious-about-your-health

Alcoholics Anonymous. (2014). *Big book.* New York: AA.

American Psychiatric Association. (2013). *Diagnostic and statistical manual of mental disorders.* Washington, DC: APA.

American Psychiatric Association. (2014). *Diagnostic and statistical manual of mental disorders* (5th ed.) (*DSM-5*). Washington, DC: APA.

Baird, I. (2014). A mindful cure to bullying.At http://www.huffingtonpost.com/izzy-baird/bullying_b_5591930.html

Bandelow, B., et al. (2000). The use of the Panic and Agoraphobia Scale (P & A) in a controlled clinical trial. *Pharmacopsychiatry, 33*(5), 174–181.

Bandura, A. (2006). *Psychological modeling: Conflicting theories.* New York: Aldine.

Beck, A. (2011). *Cognitive behavior therapy: Basics and beyond* (2nd ed.). New York: Guilford Press.

Belfield, C., et al. (2015). *The economic value of social and emotional learning.* Center for Benefit-Cost Studies in Education, Teachers College, Columbia University. cbcse.org

Benson, H. (1984). *The relaxation response.* New York: Penguin.

Benson, H. (1985). *Beyond the relaxation response.* New York: Penguin.

Bierce, A. (2014). *The cynic's dictionary.* London: The Big Nest.

Boulton, M.J., Hardcastle, K., Down, J., Fowles, J., & Simmonds, J.A. (2014). A comparison of preservice teachers' responses to cyber versus traditional bullying scenarios: Similarities and differences and implications for practice. *Journal of Teacher Education, 65*(2), 145–155.

Bradley, J., et al. (2014). Sound and fury: Understanding post-traumatic stress disorder. At hms.harvard.edu/sites/default/files/assets/.../April%2010% 20PTSD.pdf

Brion-Meisels, S. (2013). *SEL in Massachusetts: Context, connections, challenges & opportunities*. Wellesley, MA: SAM.

Bronfenbrenner, U. (1994). Ecological models of human development. In *International Encyclopedia of Education*, vol. 3 (2nd ed.) (pp. 1643–1647). Oxford: Elsevier.

Brooks, D. (2006). *Neuroscience and Sociology*. At audible.com/pd/Live-Events/ David-Brooks-Neuroscience-and-SociologyAudiobook/B00WGZ7KFA/ ref=a_search_c4_1_3_srTtl?qid=1448339983&sr=1-3

Brooks, D. (2011). *IMHO. New York Times*, June 5.

Brooks, D. (2014). *The organization kid*. The Atlantic Monthly Group, http://www. theatlantic.com/magazine/archive/2001/04/the-organization-kid/302164/

Brunner, T. (2014).Teach your child to be competitive to ready them for the arena of life. At http://www.doctorbrunner.com/teach-your-child-to-be-competitive-to-ready-them-for-the-arena-of-life/#sthash.HtNbXxnJ.dpuf

Burton, D., & Raedeke, T. (2014). Coaches key in making competition a positive or negative sport experience for athletes. At http://www.humankinetics.com/ excerpts/excerpts/coaches-key-in-making-competition-a-positive-or-negative-sport-experience-for-athletes

CAD. (2014). Attachment theory. At https://www.mentalhelp.net/poc/view_doc. php?type=doc&id=10105&cn=28

CASEL. (2014). Recent programs. http://www.casel.org/

Center for the Study of Social Policy. (2014). *Cognitive and social-emotional competence in youth*. Washington, DC: CSSP.

Clarebout, G., Horz, H., & Schnotz, W. (2010). The relations between self-regulation and the embedding of support in learning environments. *Educational Technology Research and Development, 58*(5), 573–587.

Cleary, T., & Chen, P. (2009). Self-regulation, motivation, and math achievement in middle school: Variations across grade level and math context. *School Psychology, 47*(5), 291–314.

Cohen, J. (2006). Social, emotional, ethical and academic education: Creating a climate for learning, participation in democracy, and well-being. *Harvard Educational Review, 76*(2), 201–237.

Cohen, J. (Ed.). (2011). *Caring classrooms, intelligent schools: The social emotional education of young children*. New York: Teachers College Press.

Coleman. J. (1961). *The adolescent society.* Glencoe, IL: The Free Press.

Coscarelli, J. (2013). David Brooks teaching writings by David Brooks in Yale course on humility (Jan. 15). At nymag.com/daily/intelligencer/2013/01/david-brooks-defends-yale-course-on-humility.html, p. 1.

Csikszentmihalyi, C. (2009). *Flow.* New York: Harper.

Cyber Bullies. (2013). At http://www.beinggirl.com/article/cyber-bullies/

Dacey, J. (Ed.). (1980). *Where the world is.* Glenview, IL: Goodyear.

Dacey, J. (1989a). *Fundamentals of creative thinking.* Lexington, MA: D. C. Heath/Lexington Books.

Dacey, J. (1989b). Peak periods of creative growth across the life span. *Journal of Creative Behavior, 23*(4), 224–247.

Dacey, J. (1989c). Discriminating characteristics of the families of highly creative adolescents. *Journal of Creative Behavior, 23* (4), 263–271.

Dacey, J. (2011a). A history of the concept of creativity. In H. Gardner & R. Sternberg (Eds.) *Encyclopedia of creativity*, 3 vols. (2nd ed.). San Francisco: Academic Press.

Dacey, J. (2011b). Child safety: Doing the most you can to keep your kids safe. *Parent Guide News.* At parentguidenews.com/Catalog/Toddler/ChildSafety

Dacey, J. (2015). Historical conceptions of creativity. *Modules on Science Direct.* At sciencedirect.com

Dacey, J., Amara, D., & Seavey, G. (1993). Reducing dropout rate in inner-city middle school children through instruction in self-control. *Research on Middle Level Education, 202* (Winter), 91–103.

Dacey, J., & Conklin, W. (2013). *Creativity and the standards.* Huntington Beach, CA: TCM/Shell.

Dacey, J., deSalvatore, L., & Robinson, J. (1997). The results of teaching middle school students two relaxation techniques as part of a conflict prevention program. *Research on Middle Level Education, 20*(2), 91–102.

Dacey, J., & Fiore, L. (2000). *Your anxious child.* San Francisco: Jossey-Bass/John Wiley & Sons, Inc.

Dacey, J., & Fiore, L. (2006). *The safe child handbook: How to protect your family and cope with anxiety in a threat-filled world.* Hoboken, NJ: John Wiley & Sons, Inc.

Dacey, J., Fiore, L., & Brion-Meisels, S. (2016). *Your anxious child.* Chichester, UK: Houghton Mifflin/John Wiley & Sons Inc./Blackstone.

Dacey, J., Kenny, M., & Margolis, D. (2008). *Adolescent development* (3rd ed.). New York: Thompson.

Dacey, J., & Lennon, K. (1998). *Understanding creativity: The interplay of biological, psychological and social factors.* San Francisco: Jossey-Bass.

Dacey, J., & Packer, A. (1992). *The nurturing parent.* New York: Simon & Schuster.

Dacey, J., & Ripple. R. (1969). Relationships of some adolescent characteristics and verbal creativity. *Psychology in the Schools, 6*(3), 321–324.

Dacey, J., Travers, J., & Fiore, L. (2009). *Human development across the lifespan* (7th Ed.). New York: McGraw-Hill.

Dacey, J., & Weygint, L. (2002). *The joyful family*. San Francisco: Conari.

Dalai Lama, & Norman, A. (2011). *Beyond religion: Ethics for a whole world*. New York: Houghton Mifflin Harcourt.

Darley, J.M., & Batson, C.D. (1973). "From Jerusalem to Jericho": A study of situational and dispositional variables in helping behavior. *Journal of Personality & Social Psychology, 27*(1), 100–108.

Darling-Hammond, L. (2015). Speakers and presenters. *Teaching & learning* (March). At http://teachingandlearning2015.org/speaker/linda-darling-hammond/

Das, K. (2013). *The quantum guide to life: How the laws of physics explain our lives from laziness to love*. New York: Skyhorse.

Dead Poets Society (2011). Online video clip at YouTube.com. 11 March.

deBono, E. (1993). *Teach your child how to think*. New York: Viking.

deBruin, A.B., Thiede, K.W., & Camp, G. (2011). Generating keywords improves metacomprehension and self-regulation in elementary and middle school children. *Journal of Experimental Child Psychology, 109*(3), 294–310.

Developmental Psychology.org. (2014). Diana Baumrind's prototypical descriptions of three parenting styles. At http://devpsy.org/teaching/parent/baumrind_styles.html

Doucette, L. (2012). *Instructor's manual for teaching Livesmart*. New York: McGraw-Hill.

Durlak, J., et al. (2011). The impact of enhancing students' social and emotional learning: A meta-analysis of school-based universal interventions. *Child Development, 82*(1), 405–432.

Dweck, C. (2006). *Mindset: The new psychology of success*. New York: Random House.

Education World. (2014). Ten activities to improve students' self-concepts. At http://www.educationworld.com/lesson/lesson/lesson085.shtml

Elias, M.J. (2003). *Academic and social-emotional learning*. Brussels, Belgium: International Academy of Education.

Elstad, E., & Turmo, A. (2010). Students' self-regulation and teachers' influence in science: Interplay between ethnicity and gender. *Research in Science & Technological Education, 28*(3), 249–260.

Engel, S. (2015). 7 things every kid should master. *Boston Globe* (Feb. 26).

English, B. (2014). Workplace bullies. *Boston Globe* (July 29), p. 12G.

Flannick, J. (2013). Mindfulness class aims to reduce bullying. At http://www.sfgate.com/education/article/Mindfulness-class-aims-to-reduce-bullying-4469636.php

Freire, P. (2000). *Pedagogy of the oppressed*. New York: Bloomsbury.

Freud Psychoanalysis. (2014). *Defense mechanisms.* At freudpsychoanalysis.com/defense-mechanisms/

Frost, R. (1916). *The road not taken. Mountain Interval.* New York: Henry Holt.

Galinsky, E. (2010). *Mind in the making.* New York: HarperCollins.

Gardner, H. (1995). *How kids are smart: Multiple intelligences in the classroom—administrators' version.* National Professional Resources.

Gardner, H., Csikszentmihalyi, M., & Damon, W. (2001). *Good work: When excellence and ethics meet.* New York: Basic Books.

Gilbert, I. (2014). *Independent thinking.* Carmarthen, UK: Independent Thinking Press.

Gladwell, M. (2005). *Blink: The power of thinking without thinking.* New York: Back Bay Books.

Goleman, D. (1996). Emotional intelligence: Why it can matter more than IQ. *Learning, 24*(6), 49–50.

Goleman, D. (2005). *Emotional intelligence.* New York: Bantam Books.

Goleman, D. (2015). *A force for good: The Dalai Lama's vision for our world.* New York: Random House.

Goleman, D., Boyatzis, R., & McKee, A. (2013). *Primal leadership: Unleashing the power of emotional intelligence.* Cambridge, MA: Harvard Press.

Greenfield, K. (2011). *The myth of choice: Personal responsibility in a world of limits.* New Haven: Yale University Press.

Gurr, T.A. (2013). All things education (Web log comment), July 27. At https://allthingslearning.wordpress.com/tag/ian-gilbert/

Hallowell, E.M. (2002). *The childhood roots of adult happiness: Five steps to help kids create and sustain lifelong joy.* New York: Ballantine Books.

Hamlin, J.K., Wynn, K., & Bloom, P. (2007). Social evaluation by preverbal infants. *Nature, 450,* 557–559.

Haney, W., Russell, M., & Bebell, D. (2004). Drawing on education: Using drawings to document schooling and support change. *Harvard Educational Review, 74*(3), 241–272.

Hatter, K. (2014). Children's games & activities to learn humility. At http://everydaylife.globalpost.com/childrens-games-activities-learn-humility-13877.html

Henkes, K. (1991). *Chrysanthemum.* New York: Greenwillow Books.

Human Resourcefulness. (2014). At http://humanresourcefulness.net/Cypress College/docs/HUSR224/Johari_Window_Questionnaire-package.pdf

James, W. (2007). *The principles of psychology,* vol. 1. New York: Cosimo.

Johnson, D., & Johnson, R. (1978). Cooperative, competitive and individualistic learning styles. *Journal of Research and Development in Education, 12*(1), 3–15.

Johnson, D., Johnson, R., & Holubec, C. (1998). *Cooperation in the classroom.* Edina, MN: Interaction Books.

Johnson, D., Johnson, R., & Stamme, B. (2000). *Cooperative learning methods: A meta-analysis.* Minneapolis, MN: University of Minnesota Press.

Johnson, R., & Johnson. D. (2014). An overview of cooperative learning. At www. campbell.edu/content/662/overviewpaper.html

Kabat-Zinn, J. (1990/2013). *Full catastrophe living: Using the wisdom of your body and mind to face stress, pain, and illness.* New York: Bantam Books.

Kahn, J. (2013). Can emotional intelligence be taught? *New York Times* (Sept. 21).

Kawasaki, G. (2015). How to be a mensch. At http://guykawasaki.com/how_to_be_a_men/

Keltner, D., Oatley, K., & Jenkins, J. (2013). *Understanding emotions* (3rd ed.). Chichester, UK: John Wiley & Sons, Ltd.

Kim, K.H. (2010). The creativity crisis in the United States. *Online Encyclopedia Britannica.* www.britannica.com

Kolovelonis, A., Goudas, M., & Dermitzaki, I. (2011). The effect of different goals and self-recording on self-regulation of learning a motor skill in a physical education setting. *Learning and instruction, 21*(3), 355–364.

Kurzweil, R. (2006). *The singularity is near.* New York: Viking.

Kurzweil, R. (2012). *How to create a mind: The secret of human thought revealed.* Audiobook. Brilliance Audio.

Labuhn, A.S., Zimmerman, B.J., & Hasselhorn, M. (2010). Enhancing students' self-regulation and mathematics performance: The influence of feedback and self-evaluative standards. *Metacognition and learning, 5*(2), 173–194.

Langer, E. (2014, December 1). Mindfulness and the power of thought. *The Diane Rehm Show*, WAMU via National Public Radio. At http:/ thedianerehmshow. org/shows/2014-12-01/ellen_langer_mindfulnessand_the_power_of_thought

LeButt, C. (2013). Empowering your students for the 21st century. At www.empowering-yourstudents.com/.../Empower_Student_low_res.pdf

Lerner, H.G. (1985). *The dance of anger: A woman's guide to changing the patterns of intimate relationships.* New York: Harper & Row.

Levine, B. (2013). Why the rise of mental illness? Pathologizing normal, adverse drug effects, and a peculiar rebellion. *Science, Psychiatry and Community.* At http://www.madinamerica.com/2013/07/why-the-dramatic-rise-of-mental-illness-diseasing-normal-behaviors-drug-adverse-effects-and-a-peculiar-rebellion/

Logue A.W. (1988). Research on self-control: An integrating framework. *Behavioral and Brain Sciences 11*, 665–674.

Lu, W., Daleiden, E., & Lu, S. (2007).Threat perception bias and anxiety among Chinese schoolchildren and adolescents. *Journal of Clinical Child & Adolescent Psychology, 36*(4), 568–580.

Marcoz, H. (2015). How well do you know yourself? At http://www.helenemarcoz.net

Marcus, G. (2008). *Unintelligent design.* At http://www.huffingtonpost.com/gary-marcus/unintelligent-design_b_110082.html

Maslow, A. (1954). *Motivation and personality.* New York: Harper.

Maslow, A.H. (1998). *Toward a psychology of being* (3rd ed.). New York: John Wiley & Sons, Inc.

McCloud, C. (2006). *Have you filled a bucket today? A guide to daily happiness for kids*. Northville, MI: Ferne Press.

McCloud, C., & Martin, K. (2008). *Fill a bucket: A guide to daily happiness for young children*. Northville, MI: Nelson.

McCulloch, D., Jr. (2012). *You are not special*. At http://www.thedailybeast.com/articles/2012/06/09/david-mccullough-at-wellesley-commencement-you-are-not-special-video.html

Merrell, K.W., & Gueldner, B.A. (2010). *Social and emotional learning in the classroom: Promoting mental health and academic success*. New York: Guilford Press.

Milne, A.A. (1992). *The house at Pooh Corner*. New York: Puffin Books.

Milne, A.A. (2005). *Winnie the Pooh*. New York: Puffin Books.

Morrison-Valfre, M. (2012) *Foundations of mental health care* (5th ed.). New York: Mosby.

Newberg, A., & Waldman, M.R. (2006). *Why we believe what we believe: Uncovering biological need for meaning, spirituality, and truth*. New York: Free Press.

Nhat Hanh, T. (2008). *For a future to be possible*. Sydney: ReadHowYouWant.

Olweus, D. (1978). *Aggression in the schools: Bullies and whipping boys*. Washington, DC: John Wiley.

Palacio, R.J. (2012). *Wonder*. New York: Knopf.

Parent & Child. (2014). Alfred Baldwin. At http://what-when-how.com/social-sciences/parent-child-relationships-social-science

Partnership for 21st Century Learning. (2013). *The framework for 21st century learning*. At http://www.p21.org/index.php

Paul, R., & Elder, L. (2010). *The miniature guide to critical thinking concepts and tools*. Dillon Beach: Foundation for Critical Thinking Press.

Payton, J., et al. (2015). The positive impact of social and emotional learning for kindergarten to eighth-grade students: Findings from three scientific reviews. At http://www.casel.org/

Perkins, D. (2009). *The mind's best work*. Cambridge, MA: Harvard University Press.

Philadelphia Child Guidance Center. (1994). *Your child's emotional health*, New York: Macmillan.

Piaget, J. (1971). *Genetic epistemology*. New York: W.W. Norton.

Poirier, M.-P. (2014). Growing with children's rights. Council of Europe Conference, March, Dubrovnik, Croatia.

Raina, M.K. (2000). *The creativity passion: E. Paul Torrance's voyages of discovering creativity*. New York: Praeger.

Rifkin, J. (2009). *The empathic civilization*. New York: Penguin.

Rimm-Kaufman, S., & Hulleman, C. (2015). SEL in elementary school settings: Identifying mechanisms that matter. In J. Durlak et al. (eds.), *Handbook of social and emotional learning: Research and practice* (pp. 155–158). New York: Guilford Press.

Robinson, K., & Aronica, L. (2013). *Finding your element: How to discover your talents and passion and transform your life.* New York: Viking.

Rogers, C. (1961). *On becoming a person: A therapist's view of psychotherapy.* London: Constable & Robinson.

Rogers, C., Lyon, H., & Tausch, R. (2013). *On becoming an effective teacher: Person-centered teaching, psychology, philosophy, and dialogues with Carl R. Rogers and Harold Lyon.* London: Routledge.

Rogers, G.M., & Davidson, R.J. (2013). Compassion training alters altruism and neural responses to suffering. *Psychological Science, 24*(7), 1171–1180.

Roth, M.S. (2010). Beyond critical thinking. *The Chronicle of Higher Education,* Jan. 1. At http://chronicle.com/article/Beyond-Critical-Thinking/63288/

Rotter, J. (1954). *Social learning and clinical psychology.* Englewood Cliffs, NJ: Prentice-Hall.

Ryan, T. (2012). *A mindful nation: How a simple practice can help us reduce stress, improve performance, and recapture the American spirit.* New York: Hay House.

Salzberg, S. (2011). *Real happiness: The power of meditation – A 28-day program.* New York: Workman Publishing.

Salzberg, S. (2013). *Real happiness at work.* New York: Workman Publishing.

Scales, P., & Leffert, N. (1999). *Developmental Assets: A Synthesis of the Scientific Research on Adolescent Development.* Minneapolis, MN. Search Institute.

Schank, R., & Cleary, C. (1995). *Making machines creative.* Cambridge, MA: MIT.

Schunk, D., & Zimmerman, B. (2007). Influencing children's self-efficacy and self-regulation of reading and writing through modeling. *Reading & Writing Quarterly, 23*(1), 7–25.

Seitel, M.B. (2009). Mindfulness in a school community. In I. McHenry & R. Brady (eds.), *Tuning in: Mindfulness in teaching & learning.* Philadelphia, PA: Friends Council on Education.

Selman, R. (1981). The child as a friendship philosopher. In S.R. Asher & J.M. Gottman (eds.), *The development of children's friendships* (pp. 242–272). Cambridge, UK: Cambridge University Press.

Selman, R. (2003). *The promotion of social awareness.* New York: Russell Sage Foundation,

Shapiro, D., et al. (1993). A psychological "sense-of-control" profile of patients with anorexia nervosa and bulimia nervosa. *Psychological Reports, 73*, 531–541.

Shriver, T., & Buffett, J. (2015). The uncommon core. In J. Durlak et al. (eds.), *Handbook of social and emotional learning: Research and practice* (pp. xv–xvi). New York: Guilford Press.

Simons, S. (1995). *Values clarification.* New York: Grand Central.

Slavin, R. (2011). Why use cooperative learning? *Starting Point: Teaching Entry Level Geoscience.* At http://serc.carleton.edu/introgeo/cooperative/whyuse.html

Smith-Acuña, S. (2010). *Family therapy systems theory in action: Applications to individual, couple, and family therapy.* Hoboken, NJ: John Wiley & Sons, Inc.

Sonnenberg, F. (2014). *Follow your conscience: Make a difference in your life & in the lives of others.* Amazon Digital Services.

Sonuga-Barke, E. (1989). The development of adaptive choice in a self-control paradigm. *Journal of the Experimental Analysis of Behavior, 51*(1), 77–85.

Stamopoulos, Elizabeth. (2012). Reframing early childhood leadership. *Australasian Journal of Early Childhood, 37*(2), 42–48.

Sternberg, R.J., & Lubart, T.I. (1995). *Defying the crowd.* New York: Free Press.

Stevens, T. (2015). The case for being a generous leader: Are you a generous leader or a selfish one? At http://www.fastcompany.com/3043572/

Stone, D., Patton, B., & Heen, S. (1999). *Difficult conversations: How to discuss what matters most.* New York: Penguin Books.

Stosny, S. (2015). Anger in the age of entitlement: Cleaning up emotional pollution. At https://www.psychologytoday.com/blog/anger-in-the-age-entitlement/201110/self-regulation

Strauss, V. (2014). Kindergarten teacher: My job is now about tests and data—not children. I quit. *Washington Post* (March 23).

Teaching and Learning Research Programme. (2014). Effective learning and teaching in UK higher education. At http://www.tlrp.org/pub/documents/UKHEfinal.pdf

Tencati, A., & Zsolnai, L. (2009). The collaborative enterprise. *Journal of Business Ethics, 85*(3), 367–376.

Thed, M. (2013). Pupils and parents warned over social networking website linked to teen abuse. At http://www.dailymail.co.uk/news/article-2261588/Ask-fm-Pupils-parents-warned-social-networking-website-linked-teen-abuse.html

Torrance, E.P. (1982). Hemisphericity and creative functioning. *Journal of Research and Development in Education, 15*(3), 29–37.

Torrance, E. (1995). *Why fly: A philosophy of creativity.* Norwood, NJ: Ablex.

Torrance, E. (2000). *Voyages of discovering creativity.* New York: Praeger.

Torrente, C., et al. (2015). In J. Durlak et al. (eds.), *Handbook of social and emotional learning: Research and practice* (p. 566). New York: Guilford Press.

Trowbridge, A. (2013). Are anti-bullying efforts making it worse? At http://www.cbsnews.com/news/are-anti-bullying-efforts-making-it-worse/

Tsabary, S. (2010). *The conscious parent: Transforming ourselves, empowering our children.* Vancouver, Canada: Namaste Publishing.

UNICEF. (2015). The rights of a child. At http://www.unicef.org/crc/files/Rights_overview.pdf

Vail, R. (2012). *Justin Case: Shells, smells, and the horrible flip-flops of doom.* New York: Feiwel & Friends.

Voices. (2014). At Collaborativeleadership.voices.yahoo.com/competitive-versus-collaborative-leadership-11050582.html

Walsh, D.C. (2013). Proceedings from Sonnabend Fellow Lecture 2013. At http://www.lesley.edu/news/2013/05/diana-chapman-walsh-speaks-at-lesley-university/

Wang, M.-T., & Holcombe, R. (2010). Adolescents' perceptions of school environment, engagement, and academic achievement in middle school. *American Educational Research Journal, 47*(3), 633–662.

Weir, P. (1998). *Dead poets society.* DVD, Touchstone Video Entertainment.

Weiss, J. (2013). In bullying cases, where are the parents? *Boston Globe* (Aug. 10), p. A14.

Weiss, J. (2014). Redefining teenage success. *Boston Globe* (April 25), p. A13.

Weissbourd, R. (2009). *The parents we mean to be.* Boston: Houghton Mifflin.

Weng, H.Y., Fox, A.S., Shackman, A.J., Stodola, D.E., Caldwell, J.Z.K., & Olson, M.C. (2013). Compassion training alters altruism and the neural responses to suffering. *Psychological Science, 24,* 1171–1180.

Wikipedia. (2014). *The Dunning–Kruger effect.* At https://en.wikipedia.org/wiki/Dunning%E2%80%93Kruger_effect   En.wikipedia.org/wiki/Dunning%E2%80%93Kruger_effect

Xu, J. (2011). Homework emotion management at the secondary school level: Antecedents and homework completion. *Teachers College Record.* At http://tcrecord.org/Content.asp?ContentID=16062; membership only

Yokoyama, J. (2004). *When fish fly.* New York: Hyperion.

Zezima, K. (2013). More parents opting kids out of standardized tests. At http://www.mprnews.org/story/2013/09/08/education/parents-opting-kids-out-of-standardized-tests

Zhao, Y. (2011). Learning. At webcache.googleusercontent.com/search?q=cache:USApgdtLcOoJ: zhaolearning.coa&source=google.com

Zhao, Y. (2014). *Who's afraid of the big bad dragon? Why China has the best (and worst) education system in the world.* San Francisco: Jossey-Bass.

Zimmerman, B.J. (2008). Attaining self-regulation: a social cognitive perspective. In M. Boekaerts, P.R. Pintrich, & M. Zeidner (eds.), *Handbook of self-regulation.* San Diego, CA: Academic Press.

Index

References to books are entered with the name of the author in brackets, for example: *Art, Mind, and Brain* (Gardner). Other titles are entered as, for example: *Facebook* (website); *Fill My Cup* (activity).

Your Child's Social and Emotional Well-Being: A Complete Guide for Parents and Those Who Help Them, First Edition. John S. Dacey, Lisa B. Fiore, and Steven Brion-Meisels.
© 2016 John Wiley & Sons, Ltd. Published 2016 by John Wiley & Sons, Ltd.
Companion website: www.wiley.com/go/daceywellbeing